WINNING
with
BODY
LANGUAGE

WINNING
with
BODY
LANGUAGE

———

*Glenn Wilson and
Chris McLaughlin*

BLOOMSBURY

First published 1996 by Bloomsbury Publishing Plc,
2 Soho Square, London W1V 6HB

Copyright © 1996 Glenn Wilson and Chris McLaughlin

The moral right of the authors has been asserted

A copy of the CIP entry for this book is available from the British Library

ISBN 0 7475 2577 3

10 9 8 7 6 5 4 3 2 1

Designed by Hugh Adams, AB3
Typeset by Hewer Text Compositions Services, Edinburgh
Printed by Clays Ltd, St Ives plc

Contents

Introduction

This isn't one of those books that promises to change your life by turning your into a nicer, more successful person overnight. There are no 'quick fixes' on offer; instead we aim to give you an insight into the meaning of body language and how it can work for you.

Like all human beings, you already use this non-verbal means of communication in your relations with other people – friends, family, partner, colleagues and even those you encounter briefly as you go about your everyday life. It plays a very significant role in determining how you react to other people, and what they think and feel about you. Once you become aware of the silent signals you are both giving and receiving, you open up the possibility of using this communication channel more positively and to greater effect.

Learning body language isn't quite as simple as learning another spoken language, however. You may understand all the principles very well, yet find that putting them into practice is difficult. The point about body language is that most of the signals are sent and received before either person has time to register them consciously. If you concentrate too hard on trying to control them, you could lose your natural spontaneity and start to feel self-conscious. A more productive approach is to take on board the information in this book and try to make it work for you: for example, making plenty of eye contact in conversation because this is how you show the other person you're interested, rather than because you've read that it's a 'good' thing to do.

The same applies when you're trying better to understand other people's body language. Knowing more about it will probably mean you pick up on it more easily. You'll find it's easier to observe body language when you're not directly involved in a social encounter. Watching others at a party or on a beach are perfect opportunities to hone your people-watching skills, or you can trying playing back a 'mental video' of a particular conversation to try to analyse your reaction to it.

We hope that you will find many of the tips and suggestions in this book useful and relevant, but there will inevitably be some parts that don't apply to your particular circumstances. You may need to adapt some of the advice and relate it to your own experience. No two individuals are exactly alike: we all see the world and other people a little differently.

The idea is to have some fun and, at the same time, refine your existing skills to achieve better and more satisfying communication with the other people in your life. Some people may, through no fault of their own, never have learnt to use body language successfully, however, and may therefore find it difficult to get on with others. While this book may be useful as a starting point in such cases, it would be worth seeking professional help from a psychologist or counsellor who specialises in teaching social skills. Some suggestions about how to go about this can be found on page 225.

CHAPTER 1

Why seeing is believing

———

'She seemed very friendly, but there was
something about her I didn't like.'

'We have a lot in common, but somehow I don't
feel I could trust him.'

'She has all the right qualifications for the job, but
I just don't think she would fit in.'

I SEE WHAT YOU MEAN

Most of us have said this kind of thing about individuals we've encountered, and perhaps even felt bad because we couldn't explain why. Usually, though, it's not just our prejudices showing when we make such snap judgements about other people. We may put our reactions down to 'gut feeling', or believe that we are simply using our intuition – but this doesn't really explain what's going on. When you have a conversation, you take in what the other person is saying and respond at a conscious level, but at the same time, you're picking up all kinds of other signals without always being aware that you're doing it. And, of course, the person you're talking to is doing the same thing with regard to you. The signals come through in various ways – and most of them come under the heading of 'body language'.

Strictly speaking, the term covers facial expression, gestures, posture and so on, but you also use other visual clues, including hair, make-up, clothes and accessories, to help build your inner picture of the person. It's when the match between words and non-verbal communication is out of sync that doubt begins to set in. For example, if a person you've just met is saying how pleased they are to meet you, and apparently taking an interest in what you're saying while constantly looking over your shoulder to see who else is in the room, you're likely to ignore their words and judge on the basis of their behaviour how genuine they really are. Similarly, a smile which doesn't reach the eyes will make you feel the person is insincere, even if you don't consciously register exactly what's wrong.

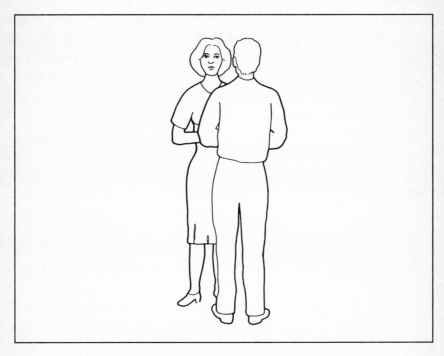

Body language conflicts with what is being said.

You don't have to be in a one-to-one situation for this signalling system to work effectively either. People who have to speak to an audience, such as teachers and lecturers, can quickly judge whether their listeners are interested by the way they are sitting. A room full of people whose heads are down on their chests and whose arms are firmly folded are sending a clear message that they're bored without saying a word. What's more, if they fidget and squirm around in their seats a great deal, they're revealing that they would like to escape from the situation.

While you already have an instinctive understanding of body language, learning more about how it operates is not only useful in all kinds of situations, it's also enormous fun. You'll never be bored at a party or in a social gathering when you can watch those around you to try to work out the relationships between them and how they're getting on together. In the same way that the conversation between the couple at the next table in a restaurant or pub is so often riveting, the unspoken messages other people don't realise they are sending can be quite fascinating once you learn to read them. On a more practical level, you can use your knowledge of body language to make sure other people don't misunderstand you as well as influencing the way they react to you. At the same time, you can learn to read the hidden signals behind what's being said to you, and develop a more accurate idea of what the other person is really thinking and feeling.

TEST YOUR SENSITIVITY TO BODY LANGUAGE

To give you an idea of how sensitive you are to reading body language, try playing a couple of simple games.

1 **The party trick**: next time you're at a noisy social gathering, whether it's a party, in the pub or whatever, try watching two people who you can see clearly but whose conversation you can't actually hear. How many of the following questions would you be able to answer?

- Are they the same nationality?
- Do they know each other well?

- Do they like each other?
- Would either or both like to get away?
- Is either trying to chat the other up?
- Are they disagreeing or having an argument?
- Which one is more socially powerful?

You may be surprised just how much you can guess about their relationship purely by observation.

2 **The TV test**: try turning the sound down on your television then watching a programme at random.

a) If it's a discussion programme:

- Can you guess what it's about?
- Can you guess the occupations of people on the screen?
- Do the participants share the same point of view?
- Are they arguing or disagreeing violently with one another?
- Who comes across as most sincere and believable?

b) If it's a drama or a film:

- What is the relationship between the characters?
- Which characters are sympathetic and which not?
- How much of the story can you follow?
- How well can you read the characters' feelings?

After five or ten minutes, turn the sound up and see how accurate your interpretations were.

A word of warning though: if you've been watching politicians or others who are used to appearing on TV, their true feelings and opinions may not come across accurately. Many people with high media-profiles have special training which, among other things, teaches them how to manipulate their appearance and body language to avoid giving too much away and to make sure they create the desired impression.

Many lessons have been learned since the TV debates between US presidential candidates Richard Nixon and John F. Kennedy in 1960. Kennedy looked good and was a television natural, while Nixon sweated and came across as shifty and untrustworthy. Potential voters who saw the debates on TV made JFK the winner by a mile, whereas those who only heard them on the radio felt Nixon had the better of the argument. No politician would let that happen to them today.

ONCE UPON A TIME . . .

Scientists disagree about the extent to which the ability to communicate through body language is something people are born with and how much of it is learned along with ordinary speech or even picked up gradually from copying those around us. The latest thinking is that humans have an innate capacity for 'mind-reading'. That is to say, we use various cues, such as eye direction and facial expression, to arrive at guesses as to other people's attitudes and intentions towards us. Damage to the brain areas responsible for this mind-reading ability are thought to be the cause of autism in children.

It's clear that people the world over share some expressions and gestures, however widely their spoken languages may differ. For example, smiling and laughing when we're happy or amused is something all humans seem to do, even those who were born blind. People who are annoyed or angry frown and scowl, and the majority will also shrug their shoulders when they don't understand something.

Charles Darwin, author of *The Origin of Species*, pointed out

7

that many of our most common expressions and gestures have evolved over millions of years. During that time, they have been adapted to our changing environment, so that they would have carried different meanings for our primitive ancestors from what they mean to us. For example, showing your teeth in a laugh was originally a threatening sign – meaning, 'I might bite you.' Or making a disgusted face might have originally meant, 'I'm about to throw up.' Even today, we might bare our teeth in a sneer which still carries hostile overtones, although it's unlikely we'll follow this up by taking a chunk out of someone with our teeth.

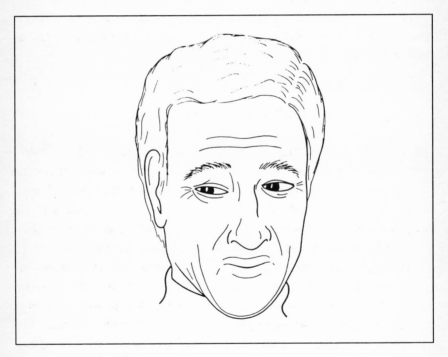

Making a disgusted face might have originally indicated being about to throw up.

As you'd expect, people in different countries sometimes interpret gestures in different ways. However, those which mean the same in most cultures are often assumed to be inborn. For example, people in all parts of the world 'flash' (or lift) their eyebrows as though pleasantly surprised when greeting a friend that they haven't seen for a while. Almost anywhere you go, you'll find the locals nodding and shaking their heads to mean yes and no – even deaf and blind people do this from an early age. One theory is that shaking your head to mean no starts when you're a baby and you turn your head away from the breast or bottle when you've had enough milk. Toddlers shake their heads even more obviously when they're trying to avoid the spoon that some adult is trying to put in their mouths. But there are some societies where these conventions are not observed, so there must be learning as well as genetic factors involved.

WHEN IN ROME . . .

As anyone who's tried to hitch a lift in Greece will probably know, the traditional 'thumbing' gesture does not mean the same thing there as it does in many other countries. A Greek driver is unlikely to stop and pick up someone he sees making what to him is an obscene gesture! This is just one example of the many signs which don't have a universal meaning, and there are others which are unique to a particular country or region. Southern Italians, for example, especially people from the city of Naples, have a vast repertoire of signs and gestures which would be incomprehensible to a stranger. Sometimes, talking with your hands to try to get round the language barrier can lead to considerable confusion. For example, you might try to show your agreement or indicate that everything is OK by making a circle with your thumb and forefinger. Unfortunately, in Japan, they would think you were saying something about money, while the Maltese would think you were trying to tell them that someone was gay! The same movement is used in other countries with yet more meanings, so don't bother unless you're certain you're on the right wavelength.

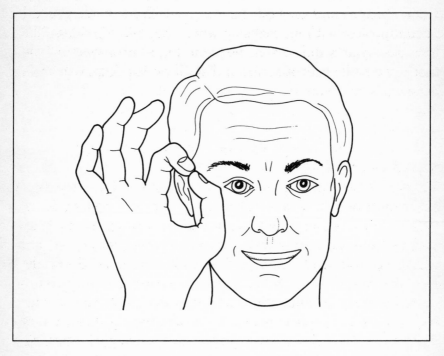

This gesture could mean 'Everything is OK' in many countries but be understood differently in others.

Mostly this kind of misunderstanding doesn't have serious consequences, but for some it may prove fatal. When the explorer Captain Cook first landed in New Zealand the Maoris greeted him with their traditional 'challenge' ritual (as they would do the Queen today). This was intended to be friendly but the British misunderstood and reacted by shooting several of them dead – a setback to diplomatic relations which continues to have repercussions today. More recently, two British swimmers were thought to have been shot by Albanian coastguards because they thought a beckoning signal with the palms down meant go away when in fact the guards were saying come here.

There are many other subtle differences in the way people from other cultures use body language which can make you feel uncomfortable without realising why. They include things like how close you stand to someone you don't know well or how much eye contact feels right, and we'll be looking at them in detail in later chapters.

THE VERBAL BYPASS

Since scientists first started studying non-verbal means of communication, they have uncovered some astonishing facts. Perhaps the most surprising is how little words matter in a face-to-face conversation as compared to body language and related clues. According to some experts, up to two thirds of the message received by participants in a conversation comes through channels other than actual words. Of course, your tone of voice, the way you speak and other verbal cues are very important. But subliminal messages are passing all the time between people which they take in and respond to before their brains catches up with what's happening. Watching your conversational partner's face, you notice and interpret the tiniest micro-expressions, the slightest flicker of a muscle or the smallest eye movement. There's no way you can ever stop and analyse them consciously, and there's little point – they'll have their effect anyway.

The fact that these messages pass so fast is important. The sheer speed, and because they are largely unconscious, limits the amount of control we can develop over them. Our aim in this book is not to turn you into a robot who can no longer

11

react naturally and spontaneously. You will always be giving away more than you know and picking up unspoken input from other people, this is a normal part of human communication. But knowing what's going on can help you to understand your reactions to other people and theirs to you. There will be ways in which you can modify your behaviour based on what you learn so that you get on better with other people and reduce the chances of misunderstandings. Equally, you will develop the ability to see through the masks others choose to wear and communicate with them more honestly and effectively.

ARE YOU AN OPEN BOOK?

Questions
1 Can you tell a lie and get away with it?
2 Do other people ever think you're unfriendly or stand-offish when you're really just shy?
3 Do you end up with all the lousy jobs because you give the impression you can be bossed around?
4 Can you easily persuade other people to agree with your point of view?
5 Do you do badly in interviews because you're so nervous?

These are all typical situations in which your body language plays an important role, whether you recognise it or not.

Your responses
1 If others always know when you're lying, it's probably because you are giving them clues – perhaps through your expression, the look in your eyes or the way you use your hands. We're not suggesting you become an expert liar, but if

12

there are times when you need to be more convincing, you can find out how in chapter 9.

2 Most people respond to someone who comes across as open and friendly, and who seems to be genuinely interested in them. Unfortunately, a shy person gives off much the same signals as someone who couldn't really care less because their defensive body language makes them seem cold or uninterested. To find out what you're doing wrong, turn to page 110.

3 The way you look at other people and your posture can give the impression that you're a submissive type, even though you may be protesting or fuming inside. They'll be less likely to take advantage of you if you adopt a more positive and assertive body language; find out how on page 100.

4 Some individuals have the knack of convincing their listeners that black is white and part of their secret is that they come across as confident and sure of themselves. Often it's not so much what they say as how they say it and it's a skill you can develop, as we explain in chapter 6.

5 While it's natural to feel nervous in this kind of situation, it is possible to learn to disguise the outward signs. It's not too difficult to control the small movements and facial expressions which give you away – more on this in chapter 3.

TOP OF THE CLASS

As we've seen, some people seem to be naturally good at using non-verbal communication – both to get their own message across and to understand what others are really saying. You may not be surprised to learn that, in general, there are more women than men in this group. Some suppose that the way girls are brought up leads them to develop a greater sensitivity to other people, but it may also be part of the so-called 'maternal instinct'. A mother needs to be able to read and respond to the

13

emotions of her children long before they are able to explain them to her. In the past, it was also important for a woman who was economically dependent on men to learn to anticipate their wants and moods, and to pass these skills on to her daughters. A genetic difference in 'intuition' is suggested as autism (the extreme inability to empathize with others) is much more common in boys than in girls.

Whatever the truth of this, it is undoubtedly the case that women are both more 'transparent' than men – that is they express their true selves more openly – as well as being better at interpreting other people's body language. Men, on the other hand, are more inclined to conceal things by being 'poker-faced', and find it harder to read the signals sent by others.

One of the major differences between men and women is in how much emotion they show on their faces. A study by psychologists at Yale University asked a mixed group to imagine themselves in certain situations and react accordingly. For example, they were told to react to news such as 'You've just won a million dollars', 'Your mother has just died', and so on. They found that the women moved their facial muscles much more than the men to express the appropriate feeling. They also found that the women seemed to feel the emotion more powerfully than the men – which could account for the difference in how they expressed it.

Nevertheless, anyone can learn the lessons of body language – you don't have to be born knowing how. The role of culture and upbringing is obviously an important one – if you were to watch a southern Italian and a British person in conversation, you could almost certainly tell which was which without hearing a word they said. Some cultural groups are brought up to show as little of their real feelings and opinions as possible. Research has shown that Japanese faces, for example, really are inscrutable, even to other Japanese. Studies have revealed that while someone brought up in Japan may have difficulty reading the faces of their compatriots, they can pick up more when talking to people from Western countries.

Acceptable conversational distances may vary from country to country. Here, the woman feels the man is encroaching on her personal space and is reacting in a defensive manner.

To make things even more complicated, a naturally outgoing extrovert is more expressive than an introverted person, and appears to give away rather more of their real self. A word of warning, though: such people are also better at disguising their true thoughts and feelings, so they can be skilful deceivers if they choose. The art of acting is all about body language and, hence, deception. George Burns once remarked, 'An actor's chief virtue is sincerity – if he can fake that, he's made.' Generally speaking, extrovert expressive people make better actors than those who are shy and introverted.

15

CAN YOU READ THE SIGNS?

Some people go through life being constantly shocked and sometimes upset by the behaviour of those around them. When something goes wrong, they are never prepared because they've missed the signs that should have forewarned them. While no one gets it right all the time, your relations with other people would be easier if you could answer yes (or at least 'sometimes') to the following:

Questions
1 Can you tell when someone is lying to you?
2 Are your first impressions of other people usually proved right?
3 Can you always tell when someone is sexually attracted to you?
4 Are you good at picking the right moment to make a point or ask a favour?
5 Can you tell if your boss is in a good mood without even speaking to him or her?
6 Are you confident that you'd know a relationship was dying well before the end actually came?

Your responses
1 Despite what many people believe, spotting a liar isn't especially easy. You're more likely to succeed with someone you know very well, or with someone who simply isn't very good at it. Skilful liars often know how to conceal the obvious signs, but nevertheless, they probably still drop subtle clues which you might spot if you know what to look for. For more on this, see chapter 8.

16

2 If you can say yes to this one, your 'antennae' are obviously very highly tuned. You must be good at picking up all the clues the other person is dropping so that you can penetrate the social mask most people wear when meeting strangers. Lots of us actually try quite hard not to reveal much of our real selves at first, because we are trying to make a particular impression. For example, someone who wants to appear as a bit of a rebel may wear unconventional or inappropriate clothes, a weird hairstyle and so on, and make deliberately provocative remarks designed to shock. Yet underneath this outward image may lurk a sweet-natured and gentle soul who is only revealed gradually if at all. Find out how to recognise the real person in the next chapter.

3 Unless you are super-confident, you probably doubt your instincts even when they tell that that someone is attracted to you. Most of us are afraid of making fools of ourselves by assuming too much unless the signals really are unmistakable. It's all too easy to misread a more subtle approach, so you really need to know whether you're on the right track. In chapter 7, we look at the whole subject of sexual signalling – sending and receiving the right messages.

4 If you're one of those who knows how to pick your moment, you'll already realise that there are also times when it's best to lie low. It's no good approaching someone who's obviously very busy or who clearly has something on their mind as they'll only be irritated and give a negative response which may be difficult to reverse later. Look for the posture that shows they are relaxed and feeling more open to the world before you say your piece. More on this in chapter 6.

5 In every workplace, there's someone who rushes in where angels fear to tread – just because they don't notice the 'keep off' signs. If your boss got out of bed the wrong side or has just had a row with a colleague, he or she will have their bad

mood written all over them – in their expression, their posture and their movements. And if your boss happens to be prone to black moods or tantrums, it's in your interest to recognise the signs and behave accordingly. We look at how you can use body language to win at work in chapter 8.

6 The lyrics of love songs are full of people voicing the suspicion that their partner has lost that loving feeling – but just how do they know? Whatever is or isn't said aloud, the message can be conveyed through the way they look (or don't look) at you, how much touching is happening, how close they like to be to you and in lots of other non-verbal ways.

HONING YOUR SKILLS

Even if you're one of those people who is already 'naturally' good at speaking and understanding body language, it's pretty certain that you still have more to learn. On the other hand, psychologists have discovered that there are many people who somehow never pick up the rules of the game and who therefore have problems understanding and getting on with those around them.

For example, someone who never looks other people in the eye while talking to them, and has never mastered the art of responding and showing interest in the subtle ways which seem natural to 'good' conversationalists can end up lonely and socially isolated. As we've already mentioned, a shy person may behave in a similar way to someone who is rude or antisocial and be treated accordingly by others. When trying to help such people a psychologist, as the first step in helping them to develop a more 'user-friendly' manner, will often use a video camera to show them how they appear to others.

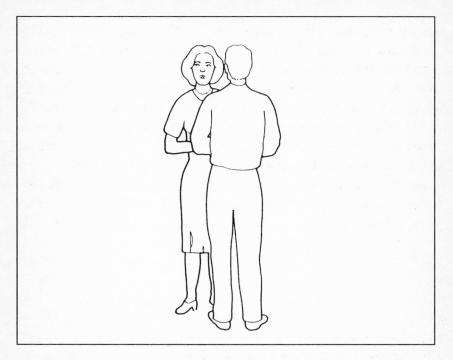

Avoiding eye contact may cause others to respond negatively.

Interestingly, the effects of a more positive response spread further than you might imagine. In one experiment, a group of people about to hear a lecture was divided into two sections. One was told to behave as though they found the speaker boring and uninteresting, the other as though they found his speech enjoyable and stimulating. Afterwards, it was found that the second group had actually learned more than the first and felt much more positive about what they'd heard. Being told to behave as though they were interested had resulted in their actually being so, while the opposite was the case with the 'negative behaviour' group.

Another experiment in California revealed that people tend to mimic the emotional expressions of those around them, and develop the appropriate physical responses to match the

19

emotions they were expressing. 'Smile and the world smiles with you,' turned out to be true after all, although presumably the opposite applies to 'Weep and you weep alone', at least in the short term – however much it will ultimately make you undesirable company.

Whether you just need to brush up on your body language or feel you have quite a lot to learn, it's clear that the effect on your relations with other people will be well worth the effort involved. They will soon begin to perceive you differently, and you will certainly see them in a new – and brighter – light.

CHAPTER 2

First impressions

———

'We can't have someone in Reception looking like that.'

'I don't like him – he's the sort that wears socks with sandals.'

'She's just a fashion victim.'

You've heard people say that 'you can't judge a book by the cover', and you may even believe it. Nevertheless, that is exactly what we all do most of the time. What's more, first impressions tend to last and it takes quite a lot to make you see that person in a different way later. Obviously, before you speak to someone and get to know them, any judgements you make are bound to be based largely on their appearance and the assumptions you make in response to it.

THE FELLOW PASSENGER GAME

If you're not convinced that the way a person looks has such a powerful effect on you, try this simple trick:

Next time you're on a bus or train, or in some other public place, close your eyes then turn towards someone sitting nearby whom you haven't really looked at much as yet. Open your eyes and study them for two or three seconds, then close them again. After a little reflection, see how many of the following questions you can answer. The point isn't whether you're right, but simply whether you have formed a definite opinion in answer to each question.

23

1 What sex are they?
2 How old are they?
3 What nationality or ethnic group do they belong to?
4 What job (if any) do they do?
5 What social class do they belong to?
6 Are they intelligent?
7 What impression do you have of their personality – friendly, trustworthy, aggressive, good-humoured or whatever?

In many instances, you will find you have something to say in response to all these questions, even though you know nothing about the person and have never set eyes on them before. The reason you can make these assumptions is that you are unconsciously matching what you observe to a set of stereotypes stored somewhere in your mind. These may be based on past experience, prejudice, images from the media or whatever, and may have little or nothing to do with the reality of the individual you're assessing. Most of us have to make a big effort to try and avoid these stereotypes dominating our reactions to other people, not always successfully. One rather dramatic example of this kind of judgement was related in a recent radio programme by a young black barrister. He was escorting his client – a white, casually dressed man – into court, and was himself wearing formal 'court' clothes. However, he had chosen to keep his 'dreadlock' hairstyle, to which no one in his chambers objected. As he and his client moved into the courtroom, the usher – a middle-aged white woman – tried kindly to steer the barrister towards the dock and his client towards the area reserved for the members of the legal profession. She apologised profusely when her mistake was pointed out, and the barrister accepted that her behaviour was reasonable in the light of her experience. She'd never before encountered a black lawyer with dreadlocks, but had seen plenty of young black men with that hairstyle on trial.

The problem with basing your judgement of other people on these kind of preconceived ideas is that they may obscure the truth about the person. For example, if you learn that your new neighbour is a civil servant and see him going off each day in pinstripes with briefcase and rolled umbrella, you may write him off as dull and conformist and not worth talking to. That way, you'll never get to know him well enough to discover that he also sings in a band and teaches flamenco dancing in his spare time. Similarly, if you decide that your son's new girlfriend is rude and uncommunicative, you won't bother to get to know her better. In the end, she will really behave according to your perception of her, when originally she was just shy and nervous.

What gives you that impression?

If you ask people how they actually form their impressions of others, they either tell you they don't know or say it's just intuition. As far as psychologists are concerned, both answers mean much the same thing, and neither is very useful.

In fact, we form our impressions about other people by getting information about them and comparing that information with what we know. The actual information can arrive via various routes – what we see and hear, and even what we smell and feel. So when faced with someone who's unsteady on their feet, whose speech is slurred and who smells of drink, we recognise what we believe are signs of drunkenness. However, if we had never in our lives come across anyone who was the worse for drink, we wouldn't know what to make of that person's behaviour. But someone who has lived for years with a partner with an alcohol problem can often assess accurately whether they are drunk just by hearing the sound of the front door being opened and closed.

25

Even though all of us make these observations and comparisons all the time, we are often unaware of it – we say we just 'know' something. What we really mean is that we are forming our impressions very fast, and doing it without conscious thought or reasoning.

The judgements we make depend on what 'stereotypes' we happen to have formed and stored away in our personal filing system. Obviously, this varies from one person to another – how we were brought up, our education, what we read or watch on TV and our experience of life all help to shape our preconceptions. What's more, these mental stereotypes are very tenacious – it'll take a lot to stop most people assuming, for example, that a young man with close-cropped hair and tattoos wearing football regalia isn't a potential trouble-maker, or more likely, an out-and-out thug, however harmless he is in reality. Since first impressions are so important and frequently long-lasting, it's worth trying to analyse how you come across to others when they meet you for the first time. While you can't control their reaction to the image of you they pick up, you can influence what that image is. Strangers may or may not respond favourably to the kind of person they think you are, but at least you can do something to ensure their picture corresponds to the real you.

What your clothes say about you

Many experiments carried out over the years by psychologists confirm that the way people judge another individual is greatly influenced by what that person is wearing. In one study students shown photos of women wearing different day-time dresses largely agreed as to how sophisticated, intelligent, conventional, religious and innovative they were. When they looked at photos showing just the faces of the same women, however, there was little or no agreement. Another project reported that passers-by were much more likely to co-operate with a psychologist posing as a market researcher when she was dressed smartly than when she looked untidy. This only confirms what most of us know already from personal experience. You may well have found, for example, that you get a much politer and faster response in shops when you're dressed in smart working togs than when you appear at weekends in jeans and T-shirt with hair all over the place and a child in tow.

Even if you're quite happy with the way you normally dress, there may be occasions when it matters what impression you give to other people. At other times, you may be content to let them think what they like, but by taking a few minutes to answer the questions below, you'll have a clearer idea of the picture you're presenting.

There are no right or wrong answers. However, unless you live on a desert island (when you don't need clothes at all), you need to realise that your choices will have a strong influence on how other people react to you.

Questions
1 Do you regard clothes shopping as:
a) an enjoyable hobby
b) an unfortunate necessity
c) something you enjoy when you're in the mood

2 Are your clothes:
a) an extension of your personality
b) necessary for warmth and decency
c) a kind of disguise

3 Do you dress to please:
a) yourself
b) your partner or others you want to appeal to sexually
c) your same sex friends

4 Is keeping up with fashion:
a) your major criterion
b) something to be avoided at all costs
c) of no importance either way

5 Do you plan your wardrobe:
a) to have something suitable for all occasions
b) so everything goes with everything else
c) not at all – you buy on impulse

6 Do you prefer to shop:
a) in chain stores
b) where you can buy the latest designer numbers
c) at the local charity shops

7 Do you spend:
a) more than you should
b) as little as possible
c) within a carefully calculated budget

8 Do you:
a) throw clothes away when they become worn or scruffy
b) live in your old favourites till they fall apart
c) regularly check, repair and rationalise your wardrobe

Check your reflection

1 a) Dedicated shoppers may own a well-chosen collection of clothes that they really feel and look good in. On the other hand, perhaps all they end up with is an overstuffed wardrobe and aching feet. No problem if you enjoy and can afford it – but others might unkindly put you down as narcissistic or even a fashion victim!

b) Unless you're immune to others' opinions, it may be worth overcoming your aversion to spend a little time shopping around for the right clothes instead of grabbing the nearest things that fit – more or less. Other people aren't as unconcerned as you and may react negatively to your 'couldn't-care-less' attitude.

c) The problem with this approach is that the shops may not have what you want or what suits you at the time you feel like buying. You could end up taking what's on offer anyway just because you're in a spending mood even though you know it's not really 'you'.

2 a) At least you won't leave people in doubt about the real 'you', but you don't leave yourself much scope for adapting your image to different situations. There may be times when you need to emphasise one aspect of yourself while toning down another – say for a job interview, so allow for that when you're buying.

b) You're missing an opportunity to present yourself to the world as you really are – purely functional clothes say nothing about you except that you're not interested in clothes!

c) What have you got to hide? If the way you dress is at odds with your true personality, strangers will be confused by the conflicting signals you're giving out. You'd do better to adapt your style so it's more in keeping with who you really are.

29

3 a) Just remember that even though you may choose to ignore the conventions, other people won't. Taken to extremes, this philosophy may mark you out as an individualist, but may count against you when you need to make the 'right' impression – say with your bank manager or your child's headteacher, for example.

b) Don't be surprised if other people take you at face value and expect you to be as sexually available as you look. You'll need to be prepared to fend off unwanted attentions some-times and you can't expect universal approval. In a much-publicised rape trial, a British judge decided that a young woman was guilty of 'contributory negligence' by hitch-hiking in a mini-skirt. Feminists were justifiably outraged, but it has to be recognised that he is not alone in his view which seemed to many people like common sense.

c) So your friends are happy with the way you dress, but are you? Most of us need to feel comfortable with what we wear, and that we're dressed appropriately for whatever we're doing. Maybe you should rely on your own judgement a little more and have the confidence to please yourself.

4 a) Maybe you just see fashion as harmless fun, but are you sure you're not a fashion victim? Some psychologists believe that fashion-conscious women are social conformists whereas those in the top status bracket tend to create rather than follow trends. It is worth noting also that fashion sometimes sets up in opposition to what most see as natural, classical beauty – for example, wearing DMs with everything. Fashions which are ugly, impractical or harmful to health deserve to be actively resisted. The unreal world of *haute couture* was satirised effectively by Danny Kaye in a film called *Knock on Wood* in which he played a French designer who was entirely motivated by hatred of women!

b) An outright refusal to follow fashion may label you as a conformist of a different kind – 'I'm not the kind of person who's influenced by something so trivial as fashion.' Clothes which are obviously dated or even eccentric will categorise you as far as others are concerned just as much as up-to-the-minute outfits.

c) You're probably not as immune as you think – you can only choose from what's available, and you won't find many shops whose stock is uninfluenced by the latest fashion trends. At least if you're aware of new ideas, you can put together your own style from what's on offer without becoming a slave to novelty for its own sake.

5 a) Studies have shown that most of us feel more comfortable when we feel we are appropriately dressed for whatever we're doing. Occasionally, though, wouldn't it be fun to break out and be the only one at the party who's not wearing a 'little black dress' or designer denims?

b) You're not taking any risks with this approach, but it may be that you're not making much of an impact either. It's all too easy to end up looking much the same whatever you're wearing and give others the idea that you're more conventional and conformist than you really are. You don't have to let yourself be straitjacketed by rigid prescriptions concerning what colours suit your particular eye or hair colour or what styles you should wear to disguise your figure 'faults'.

c) You need to rationalise your approach a bit – what kind of style is really 'you'? Owning loads of mis-matched clothes suggests you haven't decided what you want your clothes to say about you and it's likely others won't know what to make of you either. The other problem with impulse buying is that something which looks a good idea in the shop may turn out to be totally impractical when you get it home.

31

6 a) Chain-store clothes are usually good value for money and it's harder to make expensive mistakes. However, while they are safe enough, you're unlikely ever to stand out in a crowd. You may be a good ad for the store buyer's taste, but what about your own?

b) Ask yourself whether you would have bought that suit or those shoes if they hadn't been 'legitimised' by the designer label? In a way, you're playing just as safe as the chain-store shopper, and while you may impress fellow label-freaks, others may just think you're a sucker for hype! You may be paying for expensive advertising rather than quality clothes.

c) Are you one of those clever people who can find the one gem among the dross, make a few subtle alterations and end up with something that looks really good? If not, your bargain clothes probably don't do a lot for you and, unless cost is your only criterion, you may do better to spread your net a little wider.

7 a) Of course clothes are important, but ask yourself why you spend so much on them. You could look good on less, and no one will think worse of you for being seen in the same outfit twice.

b) Cheap clothes are often a false economy – they lose their shape, wash badly and fall apart quickly. Why not consider paying a little more for a few good items which really suit you? You won't need to replace them so often so your spending doesn't have to increase if you look at it from a longer-term point of view.

c) When your budget is limited, it's even more important to make sure that the clothes you buy really earn their keep. High fashion may not be for you because it dates quickly, but don't play too safe. You still want your clothes to reflect your real personality, so be a little daring now and again.

8 a) This is rather an extreme way to stay looking smart. Making time for some ongoing maintenance would save money and mean you had more clothes to choose from. Or do you only feel happy when you're wearing something new? If you find that you often buy several versions of the same thing or that you have lots of clothes you've never worn, you might consider whether you could be called a 'shopaholic'.

b) You feel comfortable in your old favourites, but other people are unlikely to love them the way you do. Maybe you don't care how you look, but don't be surprised if others assume you're a miserly, insecure or slovenly kind of person.

c) The time you spend on wardrobe maintenance isn't wasted as far as other people are concerned. Missing buttons, falling hems and grubby clothes tend to be regarded as signs of a 'couldn't-care-less' personality and don't do you any favours. Don't be surprised, though, if less meticulous people are daunted by the fact that you always look so immaculate!

JOB INTERVIEWS – AND AFTER

Dress codes at work are generally much less rigid than they once were – but that rarely means that anything goes. Some companies still have formal rules about what's appropriate, while others may say nothing yet everyone knows that there are unspoken rules just the same. But first, you have to actually get the job, and how you dress for the interview can make or break your chances of success.

Most interviews last around half an hour but the first few minutes are crucial. Research shows that ratings of the applicant made by the interviewer after just four minutes predict the final outcome very accurately. What's even more surprising, this is still the case even when the interviewer hasn't seen the person's application form. In fact, first impressions are so important that, in 80 per cent of cases, the interviewer has made up his or her mind before the candidate has even had a chance to say anything! So much for interviewing skills.

What this all means, of course, is that it must largely be the way you look that determines whether you get the job. To some extent, deciding what to wear is easier for a man, because there is usually a kind of 'uniform' that is recognised as appropriate, depending on what kind of job he is applying for. Nevertheless, there are subtle distinctions which can make a difference – for example, ostentatious 'designer labels' are said not to go down too well in creative companies where individual flair is a prerequisite. Salespeople and others who have to meet customers are usually expected to be smart, but not so trendy they upset traditionalists. If you've worked in the same field before, you'll already have a good idea of what's expected, otherwise it might just be worth hanging around for a few minutes outside the building at clocking-off time a day or so beforehand so you can see how current employees are dressed.

Women can have a more difficult time deciding on the right outfit because there are so many more options. For one thing, you have to decide whether to dress to play up your 'femininity' or go for a more sober look. You don't want to appear either too severe or too flighty, and finding the right balance isn't easy.

Psychologist Sandra Forsythe studied the effect of four different styles of dress for women applying for jobs in a manufacturing company. These ranged from the least masculine (a light beige dress in a soft fabric with small round collar, gathered skirt and long sleeves) to the most masculine (a dark navy, tailored suit and a white blouse with angular collar). Personnel managers watched videos showing the women being interviewed which were similar apart from their clothes, and then decided who they'd be likely to appoint. The women most often 'offered' the job were those wearing the second most masculine outfit (a beige tailored suit with a blazer-style jacket and a rust shirt with a bow at the neck). The most feminine outfit was the one least likely to bring success.

This suggests that the best choice is something tending towards the masculine, though not too much so. Power dressing is all very well, but a prospective employer doesn't want a monster they can't control; the boss wants reassurance that he or she will still be in charge if you are taken on. Other research confirms that women who present themselves in a way that is not obviously feminine are judged to be more competent, interested in their jobs, assertive and self-confident than those whose style is overtly feminine. But of course, it isn't quite that straightforward because you still need to take account of what is appropriate in a particular sphere of work. The beige blazer and skirt, and rust shirt with the cute little bow might not go down so well in a social work department, design studio or computer software company for example, where a rather more trendy, individualistic style was the norm.

Incidentally, experts advise against wearing too much or too ostentatious jewellery for interviews because it distracts the interviewer's attention. In most environments, men would do better not to wear ear-rings and women should keep them simple if they do wear them. While it is illegal to discriminate against homosexuals and there is much more acceptance in the workplace these days, any interviewing panel is likely to include at least one member who would prefer that a gay orientation is not made too obvious. A wrist-watch is fine – provided you don't look at it half-way through the proceedings, which would suggest that you are anxious to get away. Whatever outfit you choose as appropriate for the situation, you need to feel good in it because that will boost your confidence. And looking as though you have made an effort to dress the part will at least tell your interviewer that you are taking the encounter seriously. Appearing as though you've just thrown on whatever you happened to be wearing yesterday obviously won't go down well anywhere!

READING THE SIGNS

Psychologists who have studied the significance of how people dress have reached some general conclusions, although they don't claim total accuracy in all situations.

- Broadly speaking, men dress to indicate their social status and occupation, using clothes as a kind of badge of identity or uniform. Women, they say, are more likely to dress either to enhance or dampen down their sexual signals. Increasingly, however, the two approaches are overlapping, particularly as women move into previously male-dominated professions and choose their clothes to fit in with the requirements of the job.
- Certain people, both male and female, dress to display their own or their partner's wealth – by donning expensive jewellery or watches, designer labels and so on.
- Many men still wear (or are expected to wear) a tie as a symbol of respectability, and some use it to convey information more directly. Examples of this include club, school or university ties which will identify them to those in the know. Bow ties are more likely to be seen as a sign of mild eccentricity – the 'mad professor' look.
- Some research suggests that ambitious men and introverts are more likely to choose sombre colours such as grey, blue and brown for their clothes. Extroverts prefer bright colours, bold patterns and generally unconventional clothes. Blue suits and shirts have sometimes been found to be associated with success in business!

- Natural fibres are supposed to convey a more upmarket impression than artificial fibres.

PUTTING YOUR FOOT IN IT

Surveys have shown that shoes play a significant role in determining first impressions – they are thought by many people to reveal quite a lot about an individual's personality. In this respect, they come into the same category as fingernails, teeth and clean hair because a person who doesn't pay attention to these details is thought to be unconcerned and careless in general. It's not just what kind of shoes you choose but also how well you look after them that counts. It's important that shoes are seen to go with your outfit and be 'right' for the circumstances. Trainers, for instance are fine with casual clothes, but most people would look askance if you wore them with more formal get-ups. Conversely, smart, 'city-style' shoes worn with jeans or on the beach would suggest to most people that you have no taste!

Some types have definite negative connotations – for instance sandals worn with socks by men, or the white high-heels which were supposedly the badge of the 'Essex girl' who featured in so many jokes. Many common expressions such as 'down at heel', 'on his uppers' and the like, reveal that footwear has long been seen as a way of assessing economic well-being and prestige. Well-kept shiny shoes are associated with high-status jobs, and the clothes which are normally worn by the people who do them. Style is important too. Despite the fact that they're often uncomfortable and make walking difficult, women refuse to abandon high heels altogether. Both men and women find them sexy – probably because they increase the amount of buttock movement as you walk which is said to be stimulating to both watcher and wearer. For men to wear, the sexiest option is thought by many women to be either formal black, well-polished shoes or Western-style boots because they are associated with machismo and potency. As so often, the choice for men is simpler than for women. Formal, well-polished shoes to go with formal clothes, plus boots or trainers for casual wear will get you by in most situations. Women may need a somewhat larger footwear wardrobe, especially if they like high-heeled sexy shoes which are not suitable for work or much of everyday life. Not only do you have to suit your shoes to the occasion, but often also to the outfit if you want to give a good impression.

PROPS AND POINTERS

Glasses – While millions of the visually challenged opt for contact lenses, there are more people than you'd think wearing glasses despite having perfect vision. Designer spectacles have become a fashion accessory, and there's no doubt that a carefully chosen pair can have quite an impact on your appearance. For one thing, there is evidence that other people will think you more intelligent. And the increase is considerable – in the absence of any better information, it can add up to 15 points to their perception of your IQ, the difference between average and bright, or bright and super-bright. In fact, this difference isn't purely imaginary or simply the result of stereotyping. Other research has shown that spectacle wearers are slightly more intelligent than other people, but only to the extent of five to ten points, rather than 15. Some scientists have suggested this difference may have a genetic basis. In other words, if you inherit relatively poor eyesight, you won't survive and reproduce unless you are brighter than average and so can compensate for your poor vision.

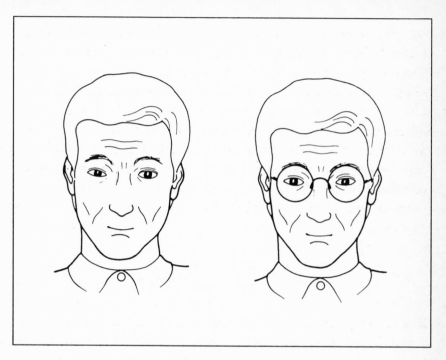

Wearing glasses can affect how others react to you.

Sadly for those of us trying to pass ourselves off as geniuses, this 'spectacle effect' is short-lived. It works very powerfully in creating a first impression, or if someone is just looking at a photo, but after no more than five minutes' conversation, its impact largely disappears. From then on, your intelligence is judged more on what you say and do.

Hairstyles – Our reactions to various different hairstyles are largely the product of social convention and so are prone to change with the times. Long hair – for women at least – is usually seen as young and sexy, while many regard short-cropped hair as tough or even thuggish. The perception will depend on the person, and there is a difference between a skin-head haircut and the short styles often preferred by gay men and, increasingly, by those who are losing their hair. Many older people still talk about 'long-haired yobbos', despite the recent trend for many men, especially creative types, to grow their hair to pony-tail length. We often use hairstyle as a shorthand to sum up a certain kind of person. For example, a would-be parliamentary candidate recently complained that she was rejected by the party selection committee because the 'blue rinse brigade' took against her. While her allegation was denied, everyone knew the kind of person she was talking about, whether she was right or wrong. It's not only other people who make this kind of assumption either, we sometimes take advantage of this kind of stereotyping quite deliberately. As with clothes, hairstyles are often used to indicate the person's identification with a particular social group – as with the colourful standing-on-end style of punks or dreadlocks among some people of Afro-Caribbean descent.

Facial hair – To shave or not to shave? The decision a man reaches can have a significant effect on how other people perceive him. Beards are more acceptable in some social contexts than others. For example, no one would be surprised to see one on a naval officer, a professor or a theatre director. Some men adopt them because they are thought to convey an 'arty' or academic image, but unless they are well-groomed, they can easily make their owner look scruffy and unkempt. And some people will always suspect that a bearded man has something to hide – most likely a receding chin! Surveys show that women are divided about whether men with beards are more or less attractive than their clean-shaven brothers.

Moustaches can also convey a variety of signals, depending on the man and the circumstances. They may be seen as debonair and dashing – perhaps the reason for their popularity with groups such as fighter pilots and gay men. On the other hand, they can at times convey a more negative image, with authoritarian overtones, as in military men, or suggest untrustworthiness, as with used-car salesmen, for example.

Fashion is a strong element in our reactions to male facial hair. In one era, a beardless man would be looked at askance, in another his beard would be expected to take an acceptable form and anything else would incur disapproval. In recent times, we've had the example of the fashion for so-called designer stubble and special razors were even introduced to maintain growth at the required length! Suddenly, it's disappeared again, and only the truly naff (or idle) would be seen bearing a three-day growth.

All these stereotyped responses are unfair of course. Not all car salesmen are dodgy or even have moustaches, and many professors are clean-shaven (or female), but nevertheless the attitudes they reflect are quite common so the bearded or moustachioed man must be prepared.

Putting on a good face – When asked, many men will say that they prefer women not to wear 'all that stuff on their face'. Actually what most of them probably mean is that they like a woman who looks as though she isn't wearing make-up – an effect that takes time and considerable skill to achieve!

Women have been using make-up virtually since time began – the Ancient Egyptians in particular were mistresses of the art. Lipstick was originally used in the form of carmine – at least 5,000 years ago. Then and now it is said by psychologists to be a sexual signal: in colouring her lips red, a woman is reminding men of what her sexual organs look like when she's aroused. Whatever you make of that, there is evidence that women get higher ratings from other people when they are wearing make-up. Conversely, going without it can be a kind of statement too, suggesting that you are a down-to-earth person who doesn't go in for artifice. You probably already have pretty firm opinions about it anyway. There are many women who don't feel properly dressed unless they are wearing make-up and wouldn't dream of leaving the house with a 'naked' face. Others see it as part of their 'work uniform'; for some it is fun – more decoration than disguise – while for others it's a way to enhance their good points and hide their bad ones. There are no rules about whether to wear it or not, but again you need to be aware that your choice will be reflected in how others see you.

THE IMAGE MAKERS

Manipulating the impressions given out by people in the public eye – notably politicians – has now become a recognised speciality. It's sometimes known in this country as 'Folletting', in deference to Barbara Follett who is said to have used her talents to make senior members of the Labour party more attractive to voters, especially those who watch TV. She is acknowledged as having advised Robin Cook, for instance, to dress in autumnal tones to soften the effect of his red hair and beard, and make him more 'telegenic'. Former Prime Minister, Lady Thatcher, is another who is believed to have employed the services of a style guru, who was presumably responsible for all those true-blue suits and soft bows at the neck, apart from the deepening of her voice tone so as to sound less strident.

The idea has spread here from the USA, where the techniques have been widely employed in high-profile court cases, such as the O. J. Simpson trial and that of the Los Angeles policemen accused of assaulting the motorist Rodney King. Tuition in body language, tone of voice and so on is part of it, but a great deal of attention is also paid to dress. In general the idea is to play down any perceived bad qualities and emphasise good ones or at least those that will hopefully benefit the person's cause. The L.A. policemen, for instance, were all advised to wear sober grey suits – the image of solid reliability being designed to counter the impact of the video in which they were seen apparently assaulting their victim. O.J.'s goal was to appear well-groomed and respectable, without seeming ostentatious or arrogant.

When John Major was first elected Prime Minister, he declared: 'The image-makers will not find me under their tutelage – I shall be the same plug-ugly I always was.' Despite that, it was not long before he was seen wearing better-tailored double-breasted suits, new (non-reflective) spectacles and a snazzier haircut. Once you know that this kind of thing is going on, it can be fun to try and spot signs of the guru's work – do you find yourself sympathising with that nice-looking trial defendant or that motherly looking politician who's doing her best to help? How much of our perception of well-known public figures is influenced by this kind of image-making? Those who pay large sums to have it done obviously believe that it has at least some effect – and they're probably right.

CHAPTER 3

Facing the world

———

'*I never know what he's thinking.*'

'*You can't trust her – she never looks
you in the eye.*'

'*I feel uncomfortable when he smiles at me.*'

Are you one of those whose feelings are written all over your face or would you make a great poker player? Some people simply find it hard – if not impossible – to disguise what's going on inside their heads because the expressions on their faces reflect every nuance all too clearly. They smile and cry easily, their faces change colour, so they blush in embarrassment or turn white with anger and furrow their brows with worry or anxiety. Most of us can't help doing all or some of these things, and it's only a minority who can manage to control their features to any significant extent. Even they can't keep it up indefinitely, because facial communication comes so naturally to human beings.

Many experts believe that our capacity to use our faces in this way is inborn, and has probably developed over millions of years of evolution. This implies that it makes no difference where you come from or how you were brought up because facial expressions are a true world language. One of the psychologists who has done most research in this field is the American Dr Paul Ekman. He believes that it is possible to identify six kinds of emotions which are expressed similarly by people everywhere, although there may be different rules controlling whether or when it is appropriate to display such feelings publicly.

THE SIX FACES OF EVE (AND ADAM TOO)

According to Dr Ekman, people of all levels of sophistication and experience would have no trouble identifying expressions of the following basic emotions, even from photos:

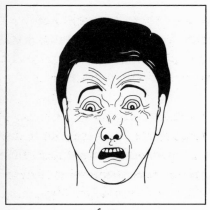

fear

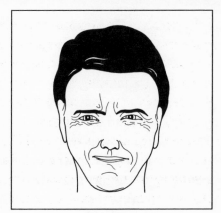

happiness

surprise

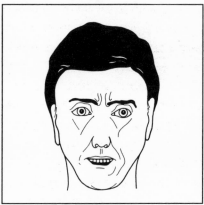

anger

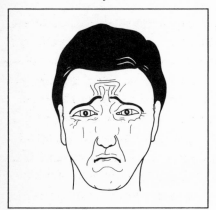

sadness

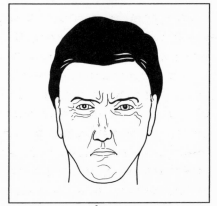

disgust

Of course, it is not quite as simple as that. For example, just because all human beings know how to smile – even babies born blind who have never seen a smile – it doesn't necessarily mean that a smiling person is happy. In some cultures, such as Japan, it is not considered polite to show negative emotions in public, which makes it difficult for observers to judge a person's real feelings accurately. And it's not just the Japanese who learn to hide certain emotions. You've probably found yourself adopting an interested or even amused expression when listening to some bore who you can't afford to be rude to. Similarly, you may have had to suppress anger or hold back tears because you felt it wasn't acceptable to let your real feelings show. Even the most honest among us learn to dissemble to some degree, although a skilful observer may well suspect that your expression is at odds with your real feelings if he or she is watching closely enough. You may be concentrating so hard on controlling your facial expression that you are even less aware than usual of other aspects of body language. Your hands or other involuntary movements may be sending signals which contradict the messages your facial expressions are giving out. We'll be looking at these other methods of signalling in a later chapter, but meanwhile, it's interesting to consider one famous example of a professional deceiver.

Some years ago, Kim Philby, a highly placed official in the British Secret Service and the 'third man' in the Burgess and Maclean spy scandal, followed his two colleagues who had earlier defected to the then Soviet Union. He had previously come under suspicion as a Russian agent following the departure of Burgess and Maclean, and was interviewed on a British newsreel denying that he too was a traitor. Although he appeared superficially self-confident, slowing down the film revealed fleeting facial twitches indicative of stress. With the benefit of hindsight, the rather silly grin he adopted after his main denial of spying appears to be significant. Presumably, this was a response to an inner voice saying 'how embarrassing' or 'what a joke me sitting here and saying things that are so absurdly untrue'.

The same inappropriate smile was seen more recently on the face of a young Nottingham student when he appeared on TV appealing for the safe return of his girlfriend. He was subsequently found guilty of murder and concealing her body under the floorboards of her flat three days before his TV appearance. Body language experts might have asked what a young man – whose girlfriend was missing, presumed dead – would have to smile about, and concluded that the smile was an attempt to cover his internal panic and appear relaxed (and innocent) to the watching world.

THAT CERTAIN SMILE

As far as its origins are concerned, experts on human evolution believe that the smile began as a gesture of submission and appeasement. When you smile, your lips are stretched back so as to reveal that your teeth are closed together in a non-threatening position. The smiling individual is saying, 'See, I'm totally harmless and I'm not going to bite you.' Today, however, the signals a smile conveys are a lot more complex.

You are probably well aware already that the way you smile varies according to circumstances – you feel and look different when you smile at the antics of your new kitten compared to when you smile at an acquaintance in the street, for example. Even so, you may be surprised to learn that psychologist David Humphries has identified nine distinct types of smile – and even this list may not be exhaustive.

Nine ways to smile

1 **The upper smile** – your lips are parted so as to show only your upper teeth. This is a warm, social smile most often seen when greeting friends or in conversation. You will normally make eye contact with the other person and use this smile as a way of reinforcing the bond of love between, say, a mother and her child or other close emotional relationships.

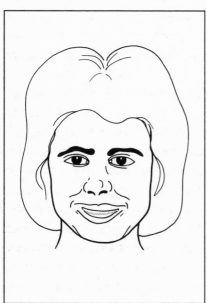

2 **The shy smile** – this looks similar to the upper smile except that your lower lip is tucked in behind your upper teeth and your head is tilted down slightly. A shy child will smile this way when encountering a strange adult, while adults are more likely to do it when they're embarrassed, but still feeling quite good-humoured.

51

3 **The false smile** – this superficially resembles the upper smile, but can be detected because it doesn't produce the tiny pouches under the eyes seen in a natural smile. You can't produce these at will in the same way that you can crinkle up the skin at the corners of your eyes. You'll see people smile this way when they're bored at parties and often in posed photos as well. It can be exaggerated into a contemptuous sneer if the upper lip is actively pulled up.

4 **The broad smile** – you bare your lower as well as your upper teeth. You're likely to do this if you see someone trip over, when you're being tickled or when you're amused by a joke. It has aggressive overtones, so this kind of smile is normally suppressed and turned into an upper smile if you happen to make eye contact with someone else.

5 **The oblong smile** – you square off the corners of your mouth to show gritted teeth. This smile reflects a mixture of aggression and fear or of assertiveness and appeasement – when you're trying to cope with a drunk, for example.

6 **The play smile** – your mouth is wide with the corners drawn up, but your teeth remain hidden. Children do this when they're enjoying playing a game, and adults when they're amused by a comedian and waiting for his next joke, for example.

7 **The simple smile** – the corners of your mouth move out and up, your lips stretch and relax but don't part. This kind of smile mostly appears when you smile to yourself as you're thinking about some funny event or happy experience.

8 **The wry smile** – this is like the simple smile but the corners of your mouth are turned down lopsidedly, almost as if you were scowling. You probably do it when you're slightly disconcerted or disapproving but not aggressive – 'You've burnt the toast again!'

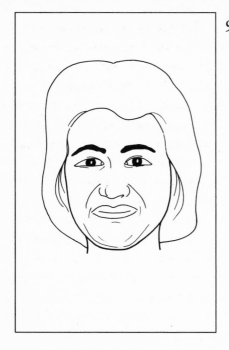

9 **The compressed smile** – your lips are pressed together tightly and the corners of your mouth move outward and up. This is used as a polite social warning – for example, to let someone know that you think the joke they've just told is in poor taste.

How often you smile and at whom will obviously be influenced by your individual personality, but your gender and national identity will have a bearing on it too. One thing is clear – women smile more than men. In general, women are said to be much more concerned about relationships with other people and more skilful at sending and interpreting signals. Research also suggests that they may smile more, particularly at men, because they are trying to be accommodating. To put it crudely, women are inclined to put a higher priority on pleasing others than men do – so they smile more, whether they mean it or not. A recent study in the USA has shown that these differences between males and females begin to show by the time children are just 18 months old. In some cultures, smiling at strangers is part of polite social intercourse. People from other countries are often thought rude or unresponsive if they don't share the same behaviour code.

TRUE OR FALSE?

It's clear from the smile analysis above that facial expressions aren't always what they seem; that is to say they may be intended to mask rather than reveal their owners' true thoughts and feelings. While this deception may be easier to detect in some people than others, is it always possible to distinguish a genuine expression from a faked one? The answer is probably no, not always, but there are clues if you know what to look for.

The first point to remember is that the mouth is easier to control than the eyes and the forehead, so the upper part of the face is where you should look for the little giveaways. We've already seen that a person who is giving a false smile won't be able to reproduce the tiny pouches under the lower eyelid that

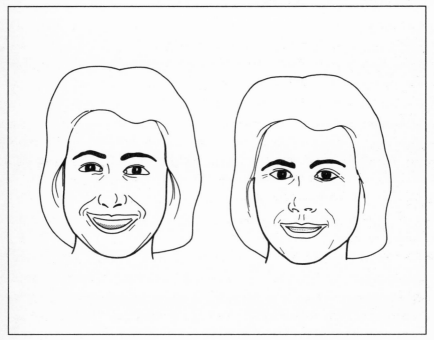

Comparison between sincere and false smiles.

are an important element of a spontaneous smile. Another possible clue is that the false smile may appear rather earlier or later than you might expect. A smile that is switched on very suddenly and so appears a bit abrupt is definitely one to suspect. Your hackles should rise too if the smile seems to be held for that few moments too long – a genuine smile rarely lasts longer than about four seconds.

In theory, you should also be able to draw conclusions about how genuine a facial expression is by comparing the left and right sides of a person's face. But you would probably need a fair amount of practice before this could be of much help to you. Most of us would find that the concentration needed would make it impossible to listen properly to what the person was saying and to pick up the other clues which we would normally register. It could be fun to give it a try though.

The idea is that the left side of the human face is normally more expressive than the right. This conclusion comes from studies in which people were asked to identify an emotion that an actor was trying to convey from photos of his face separated into left and right halves. The version of his face made up of two left halves was found to be more expressive than the one made up of two right halves. One possible explanation is that the right hemisphere of the brain (which controls the left side of the body) feels emotion more than the relatively cold, logical, left side. This enhanced level of emotion is transferred to the left side of the face, so the theory goes. But it could be that the right side of the brain is more expressive because it holds the mental 'templates' for facial expression.

Another explanation is that the left side of the face is only more expressive when the emotions it reflects are simulated rather than truly felt. Some researchers have found that genuine emotion is reflected on both sides of the face with equal force, and it's only a deliberately manufactured expression that's stronger on the left side. Psychologist Paul Ekman suggests that different parts of the nervous system – or neural pathways – are involved. Conscious expressions are, he says, controlled from the part of the brain known as the cortex which operates a system of division of labour – with different functions under the control of different hemispheres. Spontaneous expressions of emotion, on the other hand, originate in different brain areas which do not operate the same division-of-labour approach.

The evidence for this theory comes from studying people with different types of neurological disorders. In one, you tell the patient a joke and he smiles, but if you ask him to smile on request, he simply can't do it. In the other condition, the patient's responses are reversed. The patient can't smile at a joke, even when he finds it amusing, but can easily produce a smile when asked to do so. This obviously suggests that spontaneous and 'manufactured' expressions originate in different areas of the brain.

There may also be variations in 'facedness' from one individual to another, according to US psychologist Karl Smith. He maintains that people differ as to which side of their face is 'dominant'; the majority being 'right-faced' and a minority 'left-faced'. To decide which group you belong to, check your face in the mirror. The answers to the following questions will determine which is your dominant side.

Which side of your face:

- is more open? In other words, which side has the greatest distance between jaw and brow?
- has fewer dimples and wrinkles?
- do you tilt towards the person you're speaking to?
- do you open your mouth more widely when speaking?

If you answered mostly left, that is the side of your face which is dominant. If you answered mostly right, then it is your right side which is dominant. Although around 80 per cent of people fall into the right-faced group, Karl Smith found that musicians are more likely to be left-faced. Nearly all great composers, singers and orchestral players were judged to be left-faced, presumably because this suggests that the 'creative' right sides of their brains were more highly developed. According to Smith, scientists, politicians, actors, athletes and dancers are more likely to be right-faced, presumably because these specialities depend on abilities which are controlled by the left brain, especially speech and analytic ability.

THE EYES HAVE IT

As we've already mentioned, it's much more difficult to deceive with our eyes because we have less voluntary control over their expressiveness. Most of us are aware of this already, and unconsciously use this knowledge when assessing people we have dealings with. We tend to distrust people who don't look us in the eye when they're speaking, or even those whose eyes are too close together! We say that someone has 'bedroom eyes' – which may well have a basis in truth as we'll find out later – or that they have a shifty look. There's no doubting the importance of eyes as a means of expressing and communicating all kinds of emotions. Scientists have noted that babies have large eyes – and large pupils – in relation to their overall size. Right from the start they use them to focus adults' attention and care upon themselves. It seems we are psychologically programmed to respond to large eyes. Not only is it apparent from our response to others, whether babies or adults, but few of us can resist any animal with big soft eyes; a fact known and exploited to the hilt by sellers of greetings cards, paintings, and boxes of chocolates.

This response to eyes can be seen in very young babies. Given a choice of patterned cards to look at, they will opt for those which most closely resemble human eyes, and the bigger they are, the better the response.

So what kind of things can you learn and reveal through the so-called 'windows of the soul'?

● **Who's looking at you**

Unlike those of our nearest animal relatives, the chimpanzees, our eyes are shaped so that we can tell with a great degree of accuracy just what another person is looking at. The fact that we have 'whites' to our eyes gives us a precise way of determining, so we are never in any doubt as to whether someone is looking at us. How much eye contact you have with the person you're speaking to has a powerful influence on the way you respond to each other, as well as in itself reflecting the relationship between you. In a normal, everyday conversation, you look for longer into the face of the other person while they're speaking – around three quarters of the time and split into glances lasting between one and seven seconds. The speaker will look at you slightly less – round half the time. When you're ready to swap roles, you signal this by making eye contact again. It is possible to manipulate the situation so that a person who doesn't want to hand over the conversational ball refuses to catch the eye of the listener, who then finds it difficult to interrupt. Politicians have been known to use this technique in interviews, but it can be a two-edged sword because it's a direct breach of the 'conversational rules' and so likely to irritate your listener.

Once you start thinking about eye contact, you can easily become self-conscious so you forget how to behave naturally and don't know where to look any more. Some people never quite get the hang of this at all, and either look too long into other people's eyes or not long enough. Although they may be aware that they don't get on well socially, they may need

60

professional help to understand the reason and learn the 'rules' of appropriate eye contact.

● **How close are you?**
Eyes are probably the best guide to the way two people feel about each other. Friends look at one another more than two people who dislike each other, and lovers spend a great deal of time gazing into one another's eyes. In fact, looking a lot at someone is a way of signalling that you are interested in them, and most of us will respond by feeling attracted in return, even if we are not conscious of the reason.

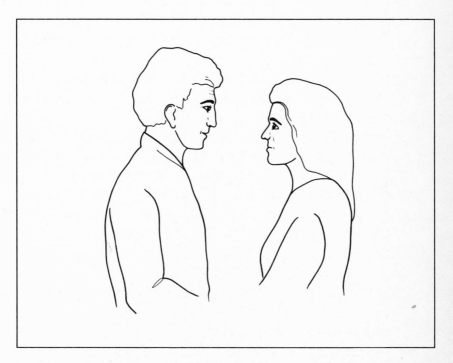

Lovers spend a great deal of time gazing into each other's eyes.

- **What are you staring at?**
  Being stared at is an uncomfortable feeling, and many people say they can sense when this is happening, even when they can't actually see the person who's doing it. Sometimes the stare may be simply curiosity, but more often it is loaded with some emotional content, such as anger or hostility. Some people use this kind of eye contact as a weapon in the struggle to achieve dominance – staring someone out is a very aggressive thing to do. There may be times when you feel like doing this, but it is a trick best used sparingly. No one likes being on the receiving end of such treatment – it automatically puts them on the defensive and future encounters are unlikely to be comfortable.

- **Are your eyes a giveaway?**
  As we've already noted, it's much more difficult to censor the messages coming from your eyes than from your other features. If you could only see a person's eyes and not the rest of their face, you could still pick up a lot of information about how they were feeling. It's almost certain that others will be able to tell from your eyes whether you're bored, happy, angry or sad, and even whether you find them interesting or sexually attractive. There's not much you can do about this, even if you want to, but it's worth remembering that most other people are just as transparent as you in this respect. If in doubt about their feelings, watch their eyes and you'll almost certainly learn what you want to know.

Bedroom eyes

You surely know it when you see it, but what is it that gives some eyes that unmistakable 'come hither' look? Basically, the answer is simple and rather unromantic: widening of the pupils, the black centres of the eyes. Although this normally happens to enable our eyes to make better use of limited light, it also happens when we are emotionally aroused. This un-fakeable sign of excitement has been shown to arouse the interest of the person towards whom it's directed. When someone senses that you are attracted to them it makes them more likely to find you attractive in return. It works even when the individuals concerned don't actually recognise what's going on. American psychologist Eckhart Hess showed two photos of the same woman to a group of men and asked them which of the two they thought more attractive. Although they were not aware of what was different about the woman in the two photos, nearly all the men preferred the one in which her pupils were enlarged.

It doesn't need the skills of modern science to work this out – courtesans in mediaeval Italy used to put the drug belladonna into their eyes to widen the pupils and so enhance their sexual appeal. In fact the very name of the drug means beautiful woman in Italian! Once you know about this phenomenon, you can take account of it in daily life. You might perhaps choose to avoid eye contact with someone you are not interested in if you spot this pupil response when they look at you, or you might entertain a person to whom you are attracted by candlelight. A low level of light causes the pupils to expand and this sets up a romantic spiral of apparent mutual interest.

Strictly speaking, pupil dilation is a sign of emotional arousal, not necessarily love or lust. So it could be a sign of strong dislike or even anger or hostility. Some research indicates that pupils actually constrict when we look at things we find unpleasant – although other researchers disagree. But circumstances should make it clear enough which kind of emotion you're dealing with. It's said that market traders in countries where haggling is the norm recognise pupil dilation as a sign of real interest in potential buyers and adjust their prices accordingly. If you don't want to give yourself away, invest in some dark or mirror sunglasses.

Another, thought less important, feature of 'bedroom eyes'

are heavy, almost drooping eyelids. Many film stars with a sexy image – Marilyn Monroe and Michael Douglas for example – have this look naturally, while others manage to create it with subtle make-up.

Vive la différence!

Although communicating with our eyes comes naturally to all of us, there are subtle differences between men and women, and also between people from different cultures. As a general rule, women look more and longer at other people – whether male or female – than men. Some psychologists have interpreted this as a sign that they are socialised into taking a 'submissive' role, signalled by more frequent looking. But it may simply reflect that women are more interested in other people. Provided looking doesn't turn into a challenging stare, it is interpreted as a positive and supportive gesture, showing your interest in and concern for the other person. In certain contexts, a woman may need to modify her natural tendency to pay a lot of visual attention to other people. If you are a woman in a position of authority at work, for example, particularly with respect to men, you can reinforce your status by consciously reducing how much you look at the faces of your subordinates when talking to them. The dominant person in any spoken interchange is the one who is looked at more, while restricting the amount of eye contact they offer in return. By recognising and making use of this, a woman boss will also minimise the chances of the man reading an inappropriate flirtatious or sexual component into the conversation.

Although the general rules we've been discussing apply to people everywhere, there are subtle variations in what's considered normal between people brought up in different cultures. We will see the same type of differences in the following chapters when we consider other elements of body language. When it comes to eye contact, however, the misunderstandings arise about interpreting how often and how long is acceptable. For example, an Italian will tend to look more often and for longer periods into the eyes of a relative stranger than someone from Britain. The result is often that the Italian perceives the Brit as cold, while the Brit finds the Italian over-familiar. Such contrasts are even more pronounced between people brought up in Western Europe or North America and those from Middle Eastern societies. There may also be unrecognised assumptions made by different groups in one society, such as between black and white people in the USA. Reports have suggested that while black people make more eye contact when talking, white people look more when listening. This can produce an imbalance which both parties find confusing – either too much or too little eye contact for them to feel at ease. Looking at people for whom violence is a way of life may even be dangerous; young men in street gangs have been known to attack an outsider merely for looking at them. A streetwise person knows when to avert their gaze.

Finally, all these subtle distinctions have to be interpreted in the light of individual personality differences. The most important is that extroverts feel comfortable with more intensive eye contact than introverts, possibly because they require more outside stimulus and a greater degree of emotional arousal.

LOOK SHARP

Unless you're a professional actor (or confidence trickster), your face is bound to mirror your real thoughts and feelings, and that's as it should be. Being aware that this is happening can help you understand other people's response but there's no point in aiming for total control. Even if you could achieve it, you'd probably come across as artificial and unnatural and it would do nothing for your relations with other people.

Nevertheless, there are some points worth bearing in mind to help yourself come across in the way you intend.

For her
- When you want to assert your authority, remember that the 'dominant' partner in any conversation is the one who offers less eye contact.
- Use your ability to interpret facial expressions (especially dilated pupils) to control the degree of intimacy in conversations — looking away quickly will discourage unwanted interest from a man.
- Remember that most men are less skilled at conveying and picking up unspoken signals than most women — you can't assume that a man will 'read' you as well as you can 'read' him. You may have to spell it out for him.

For him
- You will probably have to work harder than a woman to understand the subtle degrees of feelings conveyed by other people's expressions. Men don't develop the skills of interpreting — and communicating — in this way as easily as women, but the efforts you make in this direction will quickly bring their own reward.
- You will build a closer rapport with women if you can adopt a more supportive approach to eye contact — look more frequently and longer than you would when talking to a man, but with interest rather than lechery!
- Learning to read a woman's expressions more effectively will help you to assess whether she is interested in you so you can back off if necessary and avoid embarrassment or rejection, not to mention accusations of sexual harrassment. By the same token, you probably wouldn't want to miss a genuine 'come hither' signal from a woman to whom you are attracted.

CHAPTER 4

Your space or mine?

———

'*She always seems so cool and distant.*'

'*There's something about him that makes me want to get away.*'

'*City people are so unfriendly.*'

If you want to find out how well two people know – and like – each other, see how close together they stand or sit. The rules about distances and how we position ourselves in relation to one another are pretty well inviolable, despite being largely unconscious. In general, how much we like someone and the closer we feel to them emotionally, the nearer we stand to them and the more we turn our body towards them. Conversely,

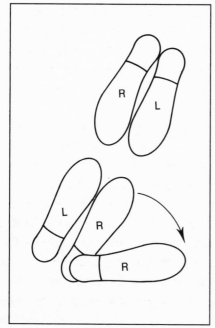

when we dislike someone or want to escape their company, we back off and turn away. Even pointing one foot outwards, away from the company we are talking to, may indicate a desire to get away; typically, our feet will point in the direction we are preparing (or would like) to go.

People who are comfortably engaged in a conversation will often stand facing each other. A foot pointing outwards may indicate a desire for its owner to get away.

How you measure up

Picture yourself in conversation with someone you know and think how close would feel comfortable. In any situation like this, there is an ideal distance between two people which strikes the right balance between warmth and threat. What this is will vary depending on your relationship and how you actually feel about one another.

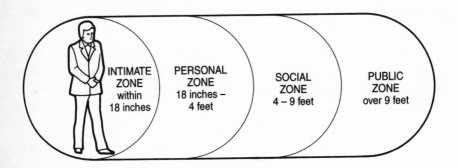

- Within 18 inches: This is the intimate zone, reserved for lovers, partners, children and close family members. At this distance you can touch, smell body odours, and see pores and any blemishes in the other person's skin.
- 18 inches to four feet: This is the comfortable gap for most interaction with acquaintances and friends unless they are very close.

- Four to nine feet: This distance feels comfortable for more formal social and work encounters, perhaps with people of higher status or whom you don't know well.
- Beyond nine feet: Most of us keep our distance when we encounter someone really important or if we have to speak formally to a group in public.

When you are talking to someone who seems to be breaking these unspoken rules, you will not only react negatively towards them, but you will almost certainly try to move away. And the reverse is true as well, of course. You need to be aware of whether you could be getting it wrong and misjudging the appropriate distance between you and the person you're talking to. They may back away eventually, but before that, they'll probably start to fidget and avoid eye contact and may hunch their shoulders or lower their chin. All these are signals to withdraw a little and give the other person the chance to relax again.

What each of us is defending in these subtle movements back and forth is personal space. How much of it we need in order to feel at ease varies to some extent depending on circumstances, time and place and also on certain individual characteristics. As we've seen, there's a range of gaps that feel right in conversation, but there are also individual variations within those.

Women are inclined to get closer to their intimate friends than men do, and extroverts can tolerate smaller gaps than introverts. Men generally don't make so much adjustment according to the nature of their relationship with other people, but they usually like to maintain more distance from another man than from a woman. A man is also likely to signal sexual interest in a woman by moving closer to her – literally making an advance. The woman then has the choice of allowing this to happen, or leaning back or moving away to fend him off. Both parties will probably be signalling their reactions to one another by using other components of body language at the same time; we'll offer some translations later in this chapter.

We are somewhat inclined to relate the right physical distance to what we feel is the social distance between ourselves. An ordinary person tends to stand further away from the Queen, the President or even their boss, than they do from someone they perceive as being their social equal. As a consequence, we regard those who insist on getting uncomfortably close to us as pushy and presumptuous, while those who back off are generally seen as self-regarding snobs.

The woman does not welcome the man's invasion of her personal space: she averts her gaze and holds her glass defensively in front of her.

The natural reaction when someone moves inside the distance we feel is appropriate is to physically move away, and provided the other person remains stationary, the problem is resolved. But movement isn't always possible, for instance on a crowded train or in a lift. We still need to do something to fend off the unwanted intimacy, and so we avoid eye contact with our neighbours or turn our backs if we can. Most people, in the UK at least, know that conversation is normally to be avoided in such circumstances, and if we do speak, it's only to make mundane and neutral remarks about the weather or jocular comments on the circumstances. Personal topics or questions such as 'are you

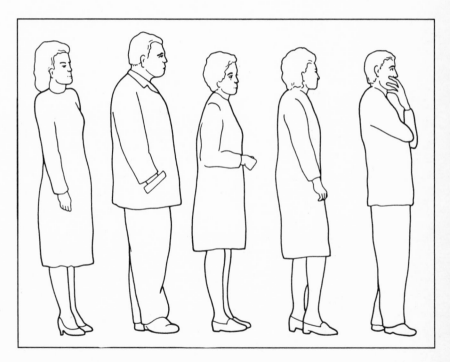

Each individual in a queue respects the others' personal space.

married?' or 'where do you live?' are not acceptable when people are being forced into unwelcome physical intimacy. But again, there are considerable international differences. These rules about talking to strangers, which are widely accepted and understood by people brought up in the UK, may baffle people from other countries – few nationalities can maintain as comprehensive a silence on a train journey as the British. But as a general rule, people from urban and closely populated areas are more protective of their privacy than those from rural or sparsely populated areas and countries.

While the majority of people pick up these spatial rules and obey them without realising it, there are some who can't get it right naturally. Unaware that they are standing too close or too far away for comfort, they can't understand why they don't seem able to get along easily with other people, especially those they don't know well. Teaching such people to 'mind the gap' often forms an important part of what's called social-skills training and is frequently very successful in advancing people's professional and interpersonal prospects.

Keep your distance

How much space you as an individual require will depend to a certain extent on the norms of the culture you were brought up in. This national variation can lead to some amusing 'dances' when two people with different measures of acceptable space try to adjust their positions to suit their personal comfort. They can end up shuffling around a room, for all the world as though they were waltzing together, as one continually advances and the other retreats.

When you visit or move to another country or have dealings with foreigners, you are likely to have to deal with this slightly but noticeably different set of space rules. Adapting to these is often important for those who do business abroad, as invariably they will be working with people of all nationalities, each with different ideas about what are comfortable and acceptable modes of behaviour. Much misunderstanding can flow from getting it wrong. People from South America, the Middle East and Japan will tend to stand closer to one another in conversation than North Americans, and much closer than the average Briton. Mediterranean people tend to get in closer and make more eye contact too, which is probably one reason why the British are often regarded by other nationalities as cold and stand-offish. This reflects the association between physical and emotional closeness. Even when you know about these differences, it can be hard to judge the feelings and intentions of people from another culture. A British woman may feel a man from southern Europe is making sexual advances because he is standing closer and making more eye contact than her fellow countrymen would do in a similar situation. He may well have no designs on her at all, but is simply behaving in a way that it quite natural for him in a social situation.

You'll notice differences too in the way people relate to one another in public places. In Britain, as in Germany, the queue is sacrosanct and a deeply rooted national institution. Queue-jumping is regarded as completely anti-social and provokes even the mildest individual into a reproachful or even hostile response. While waiting in a queue, each person behaves as though there were an invisible bubble surrounding them, preserving an equidistant space between them and the next in line. Each individual respects the personal space of those nearby. You can see a variation on this theme on the beach where each newly arrived group selects a spot of sand that is as far away from their fellow sunbathers as possible.

This sort of behaviour is a comparative rarity in many other countries. The French and the Italians, for example, are no respecters of queues and tend to favour a free-for-all approach

75

at bus stops and the like. Similarly, a Greek family arriving on a relatively uncrowded beach will park wherever they fancy, regardless of others who may have already pitched camp in their preferred patch of shade.

The relative absence of a queueing ethic in the USA is reflected by its absence in their vocabulary. In Disneyland the 'line' is enforced physically by strong rails and barriers.

THE SUNLOUNGER SYNDROME

Many animals mark out the limits of what they regard as their territory by 'spraying' various points with urine to indicate to other animals that the area is 'off limits'. Humans have many ways of achieving the same objective. Depending on the environment, this can range from putting names on office doors, erecting barriers or partitions, or personalising the company car, to leaving books on a library chair or leaving your towel on the poolside sunlounger. This last one has become something of a comic ritual in some places, with holidaymakers getting up earlier and earlier each morning to deposit their towels and beat one another to the best locations.

Interestingly, it is quite rare for people not to respect this kind of marker. However furious or frustrated we may feel that someone has nabbed the seat we wanted – whether in the library or by the pool – we hardly ever break the rules and sit down regardless. Studies in libraries, for example, have shown that readers will not move someone else's belongings from a seat or desk, even when there are no other spaces available and the 'owner' hasn't been seen for hours. Even when we don't go so far as to mark territory in this way, many of us have habits which are rarely broken – such as always sitting in the same armchair at home, in the same position at the dining table and sleeping on the same side of the bed. We do something similar in our favourite restaurants and pubs too, and feel unreasonably put out if someone is sitting in 'our' place. For this reason alone, it's always a good idea to check on other people's preferences when visiting their home or office. Asking your host or hostess 'where would you like me to sit?' avoids the possibility of the encounter getting off on the wrong foot, and can be especially important in work situations when you need to get on well with the person you're seeing. People whose job involves selling to customers in their homes are often trained to check on this carefully before sitting down because a mistake could mean they lose the sale. Employees sometimes sit in the boss's chair out of bravado, but not without being fairly certain that the boss won't suddenly come back and discover them.

'I'M IN CHARGE HERE'

In business organisations, colleges, and other institutions where groups of people meet, the arrangement of furniture and the type and position of seating can have a strong influence on how people feel and behave. In a formal meeting around an oblong table everyone will assume that the person sitting at the head is running the show and behave accordingly. The bigger the table, the more impersonal discussion is likely to be. Similarly, someone who wants to impress you with his or her importance or status can do so more easily from behind an imposing desk. People cannot approach too closely, because the desk acts as a kind of protective barrier. How seating is organised is important too. Interviewers sometimes try to intimidate candidates or even existing employees by using various techniques designed to maximise the advantage to themselves.

Setting the scene
- The meeting is held on the boss's own territory – usually in

77

their office – immediately giving him or her greater status and more control.

- The candidate or subordinate is made to sit in a lower fixed chair without arm rests, while the boss has a large, high-backed or swivel chair with arm rests, raised to a height where they can look down on the other person. This reinforces the status difference, minimises the boss's give-away arm gestures and allows him or her to control how the chairs are positioned in relation to one another.

- Most of the meeting may be conducted with the two chairs facing one another at an angle of 45 degrees, which encourages an open exchange of views. However, if the boss wants to increase the pressure, perhaps to get a direct answer to a difficult question, he or she will swivel into a more

Seating style can reflect an individual's status.

The positioning of seating at 45° encourages an open exchange of views.

combative, face-to-face position and look straight at the other person. On the other hand, to ease off the pressure, when the subject matter is potentially delicate or embarrassing, he or she will swivel to a right-angle position and look away to encourage the other person to open up.

There are a number of other little tricks that can subtly enhance the status of the boss and impress visitors to the office.

- Impressive displays of learned books and journals, awards and qualifications framed and arranged prominently on walls or desk.
- Folders on the desk marked 'highly confidential'.
- Exotic plants and obviously foreign objects to indicate that the owner has travelled extensively.
- Photos of the boss with distinguished people, showing how well-connected he or she is.

There are many games you can play with this kind of environmental manipulation if you are in a position of power at work, and they will always be at least partly effective. Before you try it, though, you should be wary of being too obvious and ask yourself whether this kind of strategy is really going to get the best out of your colleagues. They may be intimidated, or they may see through your games and despise you for them, but they are not likely to work better in order to please you.

If you are on the receiving end of such power plays, at least you will recognise what's going on. There probably isn't a lot you can do about it, and you might be wiser not to try. The person who has set the situation up has obviously done so for a reason and interfering with the arrangements is likely to be counter-productive. But if you spot the signs that you are supposed to be impressed, intimidated or whatever, the attempt at manipulation is bound to be less successful. If you do still feel daunted despite yourself, try and imagine the other person without all the trappings – say sitting on the loo or hunting for a lost contact lens.

ARE YOU SITTING COMFORTABLY?

Studies have shown that people who sit side by side are more likely to co-operate on a project than those who face one another, while the face-to-face set-up is generally more likely to encourage competition. So if you want to create a feeling of trust it's better to come out from behind your desk and sit next to or at right angles to the person you're meeting. Many doctors, for example, have realised that a nervous or anxious patient will be less on edge if they sit alongside the desk closer to the doctor than on the opposite side of it.

There are times when you can't avoid sitting across a table from someone, perhaps in their office or at a restaurant table. Unless you want to unsettle them, remember not to 'invade' their half of the territory, say by spreading your belongings beyond the 'centre line'. Leaning over towards the other person has a similar effect, making them feel under threat because you are encroaching too far into their personal comfort zone. Salespeople need to be especially on their guard against this sort of behaviour. Pushing brochures or samples, for instance, into the client's half of the table or desk will make them react negatively and be less inclined to buy whatever is on offer.

If you want to put another person at their ease – whether for business or personal reasons – try to arrange that they sit with their back to a wall or screen, away from an open door or window. This increases the sense of comfort and security and is probably a throwback to the days when we needed to protect ourselves from an attack from behind. On the social front, quite minor adjustments to the environment can make people feel more relaxed. For instance, a round dining table creates an informal mealtime atmosphere. King Arthur is said to have used one for his knights so that none would feel superior or inferior to the others! In practice of course, it isn't quite that simple. The knights probably struggled constantly among themselves to sit close to the king – preferably on his right which would put them higher in the rankings than those seated on the opposite side of the table.

The way you arrange your armchairs and sofas will also influence the feelings of your guests. Unless they know one another extremely well, two people may feel too close for comfort on a small sofa. Armchairs placed at an angle to one another or a three- or four-seater sofa are more likely to make visitors relaxed. If you can avoid it, don't place chairs or sofas so the occupants are sitting directly opposite one another. It will encourage any elements of competitiveness and make confrontation more likely.

Incidentally, if you have designs on a fellow diner, it may be useful to know that two people are more likely to have an intimate conversation when seated next to one another rather than opposite. Although a woman will probably choose to sit next to a man she finds attractive because touching is easier, the man may well prefer to sit opposite her so that he can look at her more openly. This arrangement also has a territorial advantage because it shuts out other people more effectively so the couple are free to concentrate on one another. How to resolve this dilemma depends on whether you want to please the other person more than yourself.

HOW MANY IS A CROWD?

Your reactions to a crowded environment will have a lot to do with your personal background.

Questions
1 Were you brought up in a large family?
2 Are you a city or a country person?
3 Are you inclined to be more introverted or extro-
   verted?
4 Are you male or female?

Psychologists make a difference between what they call 'high-population density' and 'overcrowding'. The first is measurable – you can say that fifteen people sharing a three-bedroomed house is an example of high-population density. Whether it is overcrowding will depend on how the individuals concerned feel about their situation. The first category can be measured objectively, while the second is a subjective reaction.

What your responses mean
1 If you enjoyed being brought up as part of a big family, you will probably react more positively to living with a large number of other people than someone who is an only child.
2 Similarly, a city type often finds the country depressingly lonely or dull, and can't understand why country people complain about the city bustle.
3 As a general rule, extroverts love to be with other people, and are much more likely to complain about lack of company than too much of it. An introvert, on the other hand, may feel overwhelmed in a crowd and find it difficult to relate well to other people *en masse.*
4 Men need more space than women and react more negatively to feeling crowded. Many psychologists believe this differ-ence is innate and relate it to primitive man's need to control a larger territory and to be more physically active. They tend to regard a group of other men as potentially threatening and

82

antagonistic, whereas women have more positive feelings towards their own sex.

Nevertheless, those of us who are used to living in busy cities will often develop mental defence mechanisms to protect our sense of well-being. People who live in cities are generally accused by their country cousins of being cold and un-friendly, when they are simply responding reasonably to their circumstances. Living in close proximity to other people, with all the complications caused by such human congestion, city dwellers learn to ignore much of what's happening around them. If they didn't, they would soon suffer from information and emotional overload and be unable to cope. Visitors finding themselves in a London station during the rush hour may wonder how anyone can tolerate such conditions – and Londoners might actually agree if asked. They, like other big city dwellers, survive by reducing the amount of interaction with strangers to a minimum and devoting as little time and energy as they can to chores like shopping and filling the car with petrol. This is why they get irritated if other people hold them up by chatting to staff or dithering about their purchases.

What all this means is each of us has to adapt our behaviour to some degree when moving out of our familiar environment. City dwellers have to slow down, respond more positively to strangers in shops and buses, and accept that country people may expect to know more about them than their city neigh-bours. Country people, on the other hand, may need to learn to suppress their natural friendliness and learn to live at a faster pace if they are to feel comfortable in a city environment.

CHAPTER 5

Take me to your leader

———

'Why won't anyone do things my way?'
'When he speaks, you can't help but take notice.'
'She's always trying to get the better of everyone.'

ARE YOU A NATURAL LEADER?

Look on any bookshop shelves or at the small ads in business magazines and you'll find countless guides and courses offering to teach you leadership qualities. Some of them are probably quite effective in passing on useful tricks and techniques which any one of us could master if we tried. Yet it's hard to dismiss the idea that there's more to leadership than that. We can all think of someone who doesn't have to work at it because others naturally defer to them and automatically accept that they are the right person to take charge. It makes no difference whether they use their talents in the workplace, organising the school run or as a charity volunteer – they just have what it takes and everyone else recognises this.

1 Were you ever given a position of authority at school – such as games captain or student representative?
2 Do your friends look to you to plan outings or other social events?
3 Do you find it relatively easy to get others to do what you want?
4 Are you ever asked to organise community events, such as a school jumble sale or street party?
5 Do others take your opinions seriously?

Those of you who can answer yes to one or more of these questions clearly have the knack of inspiring others to follow where you lead. You may well have no idea why this is so, especially since none of the questions we asked imply any specialised knowledge or training. In other words, you weren't chosen or listened to because other people knew you had the necessary expertise which they lacked, but simply because of your personality.

In order to identify what it is about some people that inclines others to follow them, we need to analyse the various components of what psychologists call 'dominant behaviour'.

HIGH AND MIGHTY

Like all other animals, humans naturally organise themselves into social hierarchies in which some individuals play a dominant role and are deferred to by others. In animal groups, the leaders get first choice when it comes to food and choice of mate, and in return, they keep order in the group and help protect it from its enemies. The selection criteria tend to be more straightforward than they are in human societies, although there are some parallels. As a general rule, it is the biggest and strongest animals who are dominant, and biology determines that these are usually male rather than female.

We think of ourselves as being more sophisticated and our societies more complex than this, but studies have shown that sheer physical size is still important. For example, tall men are seen by many women as being more attractive, and are also more likely to succeed in business. A survey by the *Wall Street Journal* found that men over six feet two in height had salaries 12.5 per cent higher than those who were under six feet.

Similarly, in nearly every presidential election since 1900, the taller candidate has been the winner. On a more trivial level, male film stars are known to be sensitive about their height (or lack of it), and always appear to be taller than the female lead – unless the situation is deliberately reversed for comic purposes. In recent years, it has become more acceptable for women to be above average height as well, with fashion models and respected actresses opening the door for female executives. Height is no disadvantage to women who aim to succeed in the business world, and may help them to counter the stereotype of the 'little woman' who can't cope without a man at her elbow.

Unfortunately, for the vertically challenged among us, we can do nothing about our height other than wearing high heels or 'lifts' in our shoes which is unlikely to achieve the desired result. So we have to compensate for any lack of natural authority as best we can. One possible approach is that adopted by Philip Marlowe, the legendary private eye created by Raymond Chandler. In *The Big Sleep* he meets his client's daffy daughter who is unimpressed by his stature: 'You're not very tall,' she says disparagingly. 'I try to be,' is Marlowe's unembarrassed reply. This actually makes more sense than you might think: research shows that men of high social status who seem self-assured and relaxed about their height are actually perceived as being taller by other people than low-status, insecure individuals.

We acknowledge the unconscious connection between height and status in the way we react to those who belong to what we regard as the upper strata of society. For example, the convention of bowing or curtseying when we're introduced to royalty is a form of submissive behaviour – making ourselves appear smaller than the royal personage. People in other cultures have similar conventions which can be adjusted to meet the needs of particular social encounters. For instance, in

Japan, the precise depth to which you bow when greeting another person is extremely important because it is a way of showing proper respect for their social status. And when Westerners meet Japanese people, both tend to exaggerate their bows just to be on the safe side.

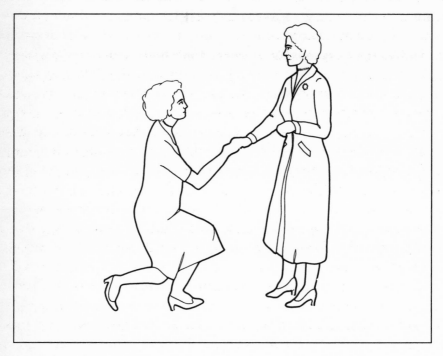

Curtseying shows deference by making oneself smaller.

Incidentally, you can sometimes adapt this formal behaviour to suit your needs in more common situations. There may be times when it's important not to alienate someone such as a traffic warden or other official against whose rules you've transgressed. While bowing or curtseying are obviously not on, you can enhance the other person's status at the expense of your own by stooping, finding a lower level on which to stand (if not necessarily in the gutter!), or otherwise making yourself seem smaller. Looking directly at them from roughly the same height or – worse – looking down on them comes across as threatening or hostile and is unlikely to help your cause.

PLEASED TO MEET YOU

Unlike the Japanese, Westerners don't bow as an everyday form of greeting, although nodding the head is a vestigial form of the same thing. The handshake also plays much the same role, and is used by some people with as many subtle shades of meaning. You may feel that offering your hand to a stranger is just showing that you're friendly, but it can be perceived as an attempt to dominate an encounter. In some companies sales-people are told to wait for a potential customer to offer their hand first, especially when they are not meeting at the custo-mer's request. Similarly, some traditionally minded men feel threatened if a woman offers her hand first, and will see this as pushy behaviour. It can be useful for a woman to remember this when going for a job interview, although she may still choose to go ahead with a handshake on the grounds that she wouldn't feel comfortable working for the kind of man who took this amiss.

In a social rather than an occupational context, of course, it is conventional for a woman to offer her hand to a man who may accept it rather passively, or perhaps even kiss the back of her hand chivalrously. What he should not do is crunch her knuckles with his grip or shake her hand too vigorously.

The way you shake hands can also convey unspoken mes-sages.

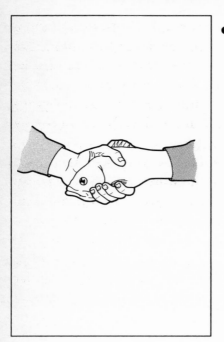

● Everyone dislikes the limp, 'dead fish' kind of hand-shake, but crushing the other person's hand in a vice-like grip doesn't go down well either. The ideal is a firm, comfortable grip with no un-necessary flourishes.

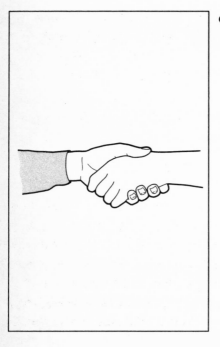

● One person may try to man-oeuvre his (and it is usually his rather than her) hand so that the palm is facing downward. This is said to be another attempt to assert dominance and control the relationship from the outset.

Certain techniques are sometimes recommended to try and restore the balance, such as stepping forward into the other person's terri-tory, but most of them are largely pointless. Better to simply note the other per-son's attempt to dominate

and store it away for future reference. The technique has a slim chance of achieving its objective anyway, since true dominance is usually given rather than being taken by force.

- Placing your left hand over the other person's right can be a sign of warmth and genuine enthusiasm, but a stranger is likely to feel somewhat overwhelmed. You're likely to get a similar response if you use your free hand to grip the other person's wrist or elbow as you shake hands – you're invading their space and they will probably resent it unless you know them really well.

POWER PLAYS

As we saw earlier, size is taken as an indicator of status, and many influential people use this knowledge either instinctively or deliberately. Those trying to assert themselves may choose to appear threatening and 'puff' themselves up in the same way some animals do when facing an aggressor. The human equivalent of the arched back and fur standing on end is standing tall, with the chest thrust out, chin up and muscles taut. This type of

93

stance, accompanied by a long, cold stare, would get the message across to most people effectively. Some of those who crossed swords with the late Robert Maxwell have described how he would exploit his large physique to cow colleagues and employees into doing what he wanted. No one is actually recommending this approach, however, and as we've said, dominance is more often granted than grabbed in this way.

A more natural way of using size to achieve – or emphasise – status is to spread yourself out so that even if you're not especially big, you still occupy a lot of the space around you. Men often stand with their hands on their hips in what is basically an aggressive posture, but which conveys the message, 'I'm ready to go into action whenever it's necessary.' When a director tells an actor or dancer to 'take the stage', they

Men often stand with hands on hips to indicate they are ready for action.

mean that the performer should claim as much territory as possible by opening themselves wide and tilting the head back. People who make a large spatial impact like this are seen by others as powerful. Pacing around the room, particularly in a circular kind of motion, may also be a way of marking out territory and clearing a space around you.

Aggressive behaviour is one way of showing that you're the boss, but an air of complete relaxation and confidence is often far more effective. This reflects the fact that a dominant individual is in control of the situation, while submissive types have to be attentive. For example, it's polite to rise from your seat when a high-ranking person comes into the room, although these days most of us only offer this courtesy to a relatively small number of people we encounter.

Posture is a very effective way of letting others see that you are at ease and feel no need to defer to those around you. Someone who is perfectly self-assured will tend to sprawl casually, perhaps leaning back in their chair and placing their hands behind their head. In contrast, a person who feels their status is low and that they therefore have to watch their Ps and Qs usually sits upright, keeping their knees together and folding their hands neatly on their lap. Having no need to ingratiate themselves with a person whose status is lower than their own, the 'top person' will usually smile less often, at least in a work situation, and control eye contact. He or she may look less at the submissive person, or stare so as to intimidate them.

The problem with using body language to convey authority is that it is difficult to do convincingly unless it is a genuine expression of your feelings and attitudes. A person who has low self-esteem and feels inferior to other people will find it impossible to adopt a confident air and act self-assured. What's more, deliberately adopting postures or expressions which are at odds with what you would do naturally will often look subtly wrong to other people. You need to be able to feel what really works in a given situation. For instance, it may be fine for your boss to sprawl in his or her chair, feet up on the desk or to pat you on the back as a sign of approval. However, you would be courting disaster if you did either of these things because they would be seen as 'uppity' or as a challenge to the boss's authority. What most of us can do, however, is to consciously aim to appear relaxed and at ease without being inappropriately casual. Giving the impression that you are what the French describe as 'happy inside your skin' will make other people more likely to see you as a confident, capable individual who can be relied on.

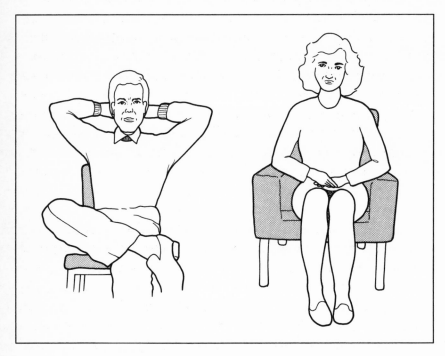

Posture says a great deal about status.

It is also worth remembering that there are some people who are natural bullies and who will take advantage of others whenever they 'smell' fear. Such people do not, however, take on anyone who looks as though they might be able to defend themselves physically or socially.

HOW TO SUCCEED IN INTERVIEWS

As we saw in chapter 2, the outcome of a job interview is often decided within the first five minutes or so. Since this is obviously too soon for your intelligence, abilities, personality or attitudes to be properly assessed, the impression you make through your appearance and mannerisms must be the deciding factor. Assuming that you have the right qualifications and experience and have done your homework prior to the interview, what else can you do to increase your chances of success?

As we saw in chapter 2, dressing the part is essential, and if you're not sure what that actually means, do a little research if you can. In general, the guidelines are to dress neatly rather than sexily (unless the job requires it, of course) and avoid extremes of fashion. Every interviewer will have their own ideas of what's important, but common pet hates include bizarre hairstyles, beards, smoking, bow ties and slip-on shoes for men!

- When you first meet your interviewer, stand up (if necessary), smile and meet their eyes without staring. Let them be the one to offer a handshake and match your grip to theirs.
- Don't stand or sit too close to the interviewer as you could be invading his or her personal space – at least three or four feet away is about right for most westerners. If your interviewer is from a culture where different norms apply, you will need to be alert to their 'comfort zone' and follow their lead if in doubt. Remember too that a woman can sit closer to a man without disturbing him than another man could.
- The interviewer will normally indicate where you should sit, but if you have a choice, opt for a side-by-side position rather

than across a desk. This is more likely to make them view you as a potential ally rather than a challenger.

- Sit in a relaxed position, with your hands comfortably apart but without sprawling or leaning forward too aggressively. Leaning back in your chair, on the other hand, can look arrogant, especially if you stare at the interviewer while you're doing it.

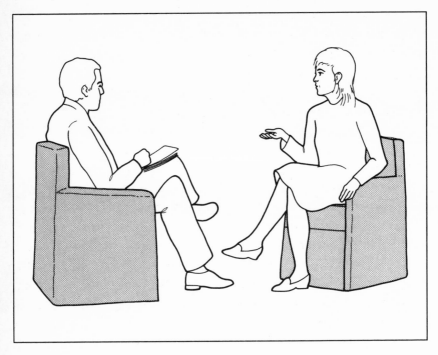

Sitting in a relaxed but upright manner will convey an alert interest.

- Even if you're nervous, try to avoid obviously defensive postures, such as folding your arms or clamping your knees together. It's perfectly natural to feel a bit tense, and an allowance will be made for this. Someone who shows no signs of nervousness during an important interview may well come across as over-confident or unconcerned.

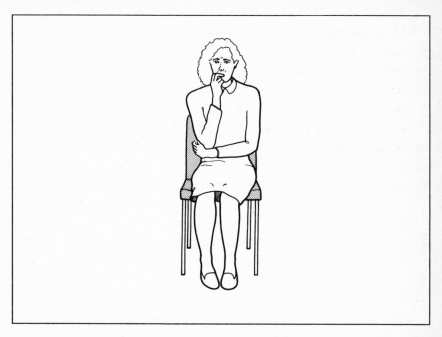

A defensive and nervous posture.

- Look at the interviewer, but without appearing to stare. Experts recommend that making eye contact for around a third of the time is the ideal, but you can't possibly calculate that while you're in there. Just try to maintain what feels like a comfortable level and avoid averting your gaze too much as this can make you appear untrustworthy. When you do break eye contact, it is better to look up (if you're think-ing) or down (if you've come to the end of what you wanted to say). Swinging the eyes sideways on the same level is what comes across as shifty.
- Take your cue from the interviewer when it comes to mood – but don't overdo either smiles or seriousness. Worst of all is a fixed grin.
- You may make the interviewer more receptive and improve the rapport between you by mirroring their body language. This means taking up similar positions for your arms, legs

99

and hands for example, but exercise some caution here. Sometimes following suit in this way would be counter-productive – as when the interviewer is adopting a challenging or threatening posture. And, of course, it would be transparent if you let it become exaggerated and blatant.

ASSERTIVE NOT AGGRESSIVE

In the animal kingdom, 'top dogs' rarely have to fight other members of the group and those lower down the pecking order can hardly ever improve their status by scrapping with those just above them. You could say that fighting for dominance is almost as useless as copulating for virginity.

It's much the same where human animals are concerned. With rare exceptions, certain individuals achieve dominance because it is ceded to them and not because they have won it by force – either literally or by bullying. You are more likely to improve your position by standing up for your rights in an insistent yet calm and reasonable way – which is what assertiveness training aims to teach. In contrast, the person who loses his or her temper almost always loses the argument in the process because all they do is arouse resentment and resistance in the person towards whom their apoplexy is directed. Similarly, people who constantly talk very loudly are not necessarily dominant, although they may want you to think so. More often than not they are simply demonstrating that they have learned that no one listens to them unless they shout. A quiet voice, such as that used by Marlon Brando in *The Godfather* is often a great deal more threatening simply because it is clear that power already resides in that individual – it isn't necessary to display or prove the fact. US President Theodore Roosevelt maintained that the ideal was to 'speak softly and carry a big stick', by which he meant having some kind of power base or back-up to reinforce the message.

100

Dominant people use particular kinds of non-verbal communication because they are dominant, rather than the other way round. In other words, you can't achieve top dog status simply by modifying your body language alone. Nevertheless, you can learn to synchronise your messages so that your words are reinforced by your body language and not contradicted. For example, when you want to make a complaint – say about poor service – you need to stand confidently, with your head up and your shoulders back and look the other person in the eye. Mumbling your complaint with your head on your chin and your body slumped or stooped is unlikely to achieve your objective. Equally useful, understanding the relationship between status and body language enables you to see others for what they really are. You're much less likely to be intimidated by a bully or blusterer or to inadvertently tread on the toes of someone whose good opinion you need if you are good at reading their non-verbal signals.

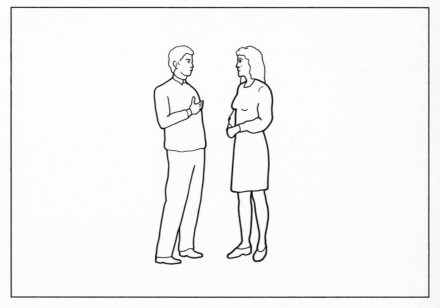

Standing tall and making direct eye contact will give the impression of confidence and make for effective communication.

CHAPTER 6

Good vibrations

———

'I liked her right from the start.'
'He's one of those people everyone gets on with.'
'I'm no good at meeting strangers.'

'Pleased to meet you,' we murmur as we are introduced to a stranger. Mostly the words are just a ritual response, a formula used in polite society as a way of acknowledging one another. Neither we nor the other person give the slightest consideration to whether we mean what we say, they are just empty words. Nevertheless, within a few minutes (or even less) of meeting, the two people concerned will have formed an impression of each other and made up their minds whether they really are pleased to know this person or not. Often this initial reaction stays with us and it may well determine whether we bother to get to know our new acquaintance any better. If circumstances conspire to throw us together a lot after the initial meeting, we may eventually realise that our first assessment was wrong, and that we like the other person rather more (or less) than we did to begin with. More often than not, however, one or both of us will have to make some kind of effort if we want to see the person again, so our immediate response to that first encounter is all-important.

Most of us prefer to be liked rather than disliked, so we need to understand what it is about us that determines the impression we make. Equally, if you've ever got it wrong – say following up a meeting with an apparently amusing individual who turns out to be capable of boring for England – you'll want to know how to avoid similar mistakes in the future.

Whether someone likes you or not is one of the most important things you need to know. This is equally so in business, friendship or love. It's possible that your new acquaintance will be blunt enough to tell you outright that they find you very interesting and attractive, or even totally incompatible. But it's much more likely they will conceal their true feelings to a great extent or say little or nothing about them, so you have to fall back on body language to discover what they're really thinking and feeling.

As we saw in chapter 2, one of the key factors controlling our response to another person is how physically attractive we find them. Interestingly, this aspect plays an important role irrespective of gender. In other words, it isn't only heterosexual men and women who will weigh each other up in this way. Women and men both have ideas about the physical qualities they admire in a person of their own sex, and will be friendlier to someone whose looks meet their criteria. So let's assume you're meeting someone for the first time: how can you tell whether they like you or not? What you actually do is read the non-verbal signals which convey warmth and acceptance. Most of us are already fairly experienced at this – and women are better at it than men on average. We do it by *unconsciously* processing the complete pattern of signals we're receiving. But when you want to improve your skill in this area it is useful to analyse the separate components *consciously*.

Reading the signs
- **Friendly looks**: even when you're simply making small talk which is not particularly interesting in itself, someone who likes you will look at you a lot, especially while you're speaking. Psychologists use the term 'gaze' to cover this and it means looking at another person – especially at their face, although not always directly into their eyes. Video analysis has shown that when we're just chatting socially,

we look at all parts of the other person's face, but most of our attention is concentrated on their eyes and mouth, because these are the most expressive features.

When you're making a conscious effort to notice how much the other person is looking at you, you may need to make certain adjustments to the conclusions you reach depending on who it is. For one thing, some studies have shown that not only are women likely to gaze more than men, but they also interpret another person's gaze more positively. Men in general are apparently less inclined to perceive being looked at frequently as a sign of warmth or friendship. In the USA, where much of the research has been done, and in northern Europe, men often learn to conceal their emotions and are less open than women. In contrast, people from other countries – such as Mediterranean and Arab ones – will generally gaze more and are less inclined to be embarrassed when you look at them.

- **Smiles**: you probably smile automatically when speaking to someone for the first time in a social situation, and they are likely to do the same. Once conversation gets started, however, a smile, even a very brief one, shows you that the other person is responding to you and is not trying to make a quick escape. Beware, though, the smile that never reaches the eyes because it means the person is smiling out of 'duty' or politeness, not because they feel like it. You'll almost certainly pick this up at an unconscious level anyway and so begin to feel uncomfortable, but it's useful to realise why.

- **Warm tones**: all of us use tone of voice as a measure of the emotional content of the words we're hearing, and can actually separate it from the meaning of the words themselves. For example, one study found that people could distinguish an angry tone from a sad one, a sympathetic from a jealous one and so on, even when the speakers were

107

simply reciting the alphabet. Interestingly, though, the researchers found that some people were more skilful both at communicating and picking up feelings through tone of voice alone. Generally, the voice is better at conveying positive than negative emotions, and you will probably pick up the feeling that someone likes you from the sound rather than the content of what they're saying. Incidentally, the researchers also claim that you can tell more from a person's voice when they are being dishonest than when they are being open and straightforward.

- **Body pointing**: if you're both standing up while talking to one another, have a quick glance down at your conversational partner's feet. Which way are they facing? It's good news if they are roughly at right angles to your own, because this implies that their feelings about the encounter with you are very similar to yours. With someone you've only just met, this posture conveys a low to moderate degree of intimacy which is probably good enough at this stage. Keep talking and await developments!

The same principle applies when you're sitting down. Someone who finds you interesting will turn their body towards you, perhaps by crossing the leg that's further away over the one that's nearer to you. This distinction is especially obvious if there is someone else sitting on your companion's other side as it is clear that he or she has chosen to concentrate on you rather than the other neighbour. A word of caution though: don't over-interpret any one feature. Some people habitually cross their legs in a particular way, for example – say right over left – regardless of the social circumstances. Therefore you always have to watch for other signs to verify your conclusions, and be on the look-out for complete patterns rather than making rigid assessments on the basis of isolated aspects of body language.

Body pointing.

DO YOUR FEELINGS SHOW?

It's often hard to relax and be yourself when you meet new people. You want to make a good impression, but worrying about whether you are succeeding will usually be counter-productive. With a bit of thought and practice, however, most of us can learn the 'social skills' which can carry us through so that eventually they become second nature. It's a bit like learning to drive: at first you have to think carefully about your hands and feet as you operate the pedals and change gear, but after a while you do it completely automatically. It really isn't that difficult to use body language to let someone know that you like or are interested in them, even if making small talk doesn't come easily to you.

109

Six simple ways to communicate with someone you like

Don't stint on smiles

This doesn't mean keeping a silly grin plastered all over your face, but simply responding with a smile whenever it feels right. And if you really are interested in this other person, surely you'll feel like smiling sometimes? This matters because as well as being a warm and friendly gesture in itself, a smile reassures the other person of your interest in them and makes them want to smile back. There really is evidence that people who are naturally smiley get a positive response from other people – which makes them feel like smiling all the more.

It's not what you say . . .

. . . it's the way that you say it. Most of us get a nasty shock when we hear our own voices on a tape recorder or answering machine because it sounds so different from how we expected. Other people won't have the same problem, but it's worth listening to yourself and trying to analyse the way you sound. Loud and high-pitched speech tends to be off-putting, and those who talk very fast are often perceived as untrustworthy. Remember that tone of voice is as important as what you're saying when you meet a stranger, so try and put your feelings across in the way you speak, even when you're not saying anything much. No one is suggesting that you imitate some well-known politicians by dramatically altering the way you sound, but just be aware of the pitch, speed and tone so your voice reflects your real meaning.

Keep your eye on the ball

Not literally of course, but unless you look at the person you're talking to, they'll assume you're bored or unfriendly. That doesn't mean staring or gazing constantly into their eyes – the first appears hostile and the second is reserved for lovers (see page 61). When you want to show that you're friendly, glance frequently into the other person's face, but for brief periods. Your eyes will probably meet just for a second or so each time, but that's enough to keep both of you interested.

Listen and learn

Unless your new friend is an insensitive bore, he or she will need to feel that you are interested in them and what they have to say. This is still true even when the conversation is only at the small talk, getting-to-know-you stage. Jumping in when they're half-way through a sentence or even neglecting 'feedback': signals such as nodding and smiling will be taken as lack of encouragement to keep going. If your aim is to make your companion like you, remember that most people are naturally warm towards someone who makes them feel they're entertaining and interesting talkers. Traditionally, advice to shy people always focused on asking the other person about themselves, and while this is still useful, you can take it too far. Natural conversation is rather like a game of tennis, passing back and forth between the two people, even if one has rather more than their fair share of the ball. So most people will expect you to respond by revealing a certain amount about yourself rather than constantly asking questions. This doesn't mean spilling all the beans about your love life or detailing your family history, but a certain amount of what the experts call self-disclosure will help the other person to acquire a more rounded picture of you as an interesting individual rather than just a willing ear. When a relationship is building positively, self-disclosure is roughly synchronous – that is to say, each party reveals a similar amount of private detail at approximately the same rate. When

111

one person pours their heart out and the other reacts by clamming up, something has gone wrong with the development of intimacy.

A friendly face

Most of us have learned to keep some control over our facial expressions in social situations, opting for a bland, pleasant look that says little about our real feelings. In particular, we are reluctant to reveal negative emotions to people we don't know well. Interestingly, research by American psychologist Dr Paul Ekman has shown that happiness is one of the most easily read expressions – people the world over, whatever culture they come from, know a happy face when they see one. What's more, the emotion is contagious, so if your conversational partner makes you feel good, let it show. Your obvious enjoyment of their company will get through to them and make it more likely that they will feel good about being with you too.

A touch of warmth

Touching another person in a non-sexual way – say on the arm or shoulder – can be a powerful means of communicating warmth and sympathy. Unless you sense that it would be unwelcome, don't be shy about touching if it comes naturally to you. Tactile people are frequently seen by others as warm and attractive, but you do need to be sensitive to the other person's likely reaction. Individuals vary quite a lot in how they feel about being touched by someone they don't know well. Some research suggests that it is least likely to go down well when a man is touched by another man or when a woman is touched by a man who isn't a close friend or lover. These studies were done in the USA and don't necessarily apply to people from other countries – Mediterranean men for example, are much less reserved and will unhesitatingly put their arms around one another.

MIRROR IMAGES

There's one other striking sign that tells you for sure that two people are in tune and getting on well together and it's called mirroring. Watch the way they sit, stand and move and you'll notice that they tend to imitate one another almost as though you're seeing a single individual reflected in a mirror. Other names for this kind of behaviour are synchrony and postural echo. You almost certainly do this yourself when you're with a good friend, even though it's an unconscious process which neither of you is aware of until you start to think about it. Basically, it's a way of conveying to each other the unspoken message: 'See, I'm just like you.'

Once you know what to look for, you'll be amazed how often you can spot manifestations of mirroring. One of the most obvious is copying the way the other person is sitting – crossing the opposite leg and resting the chin on the opposite hand, for example. Sometimes you'll notice that in the middle of a conversation you both lean forwards toward each other at the same moment or use exactly the same gesture to emphasise a point. The better you know someone and the closer your relationship, the more you reflect one another's body language. When two people are completely in tune, even their briefest facial expressions will coincide.

So is mirroring just an interesting psychological phenomenon, or can you exploit your knowledge to influence your relationship with others? The answer is yes you can make use of it, but only to a limited extent, and you do have to be subtle about it. You'll get some very funny looks if you start

113

slavishly imitating every tiny movement of the person you're with, and end up by irritating rather than reassuring them, much like a child who thinks it's a funny game to repeat everything you say back to you.

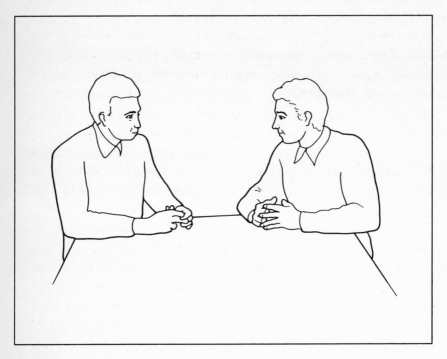

Mirroring can help to reinforce the rapport between individuals.

When it can work

- If the person you're talking to seems unresponsive, watch their movements and start shadowing some of them with your own. Adjust your posture to match theirs without being too obvious about it. They may just loosen up and you haven't much to lose.
- When you want to assert yourself, make your gestures and changes of posture a little more pronounced than usual.

114

Research shows that the person who initiates such changes and is copied by the other tends to be the dominant partner in the encounter.

- When you need to get someone on your side to reassure them, try some subtle mirroring to put them at their ease. This is a technique often used by high status people to make a subordinate feel more comfortable.

- Knowing that it is the dominant person whose behaviour is mirrored can be useful when you need to decide which person has the power in a relationship. For example, when one half of a couple does most of the talking but simultaneously copies the quiet one's body language, you have a clearer idea of who makes the real decisions. Salespeople especially are trained to look out for this phenomenon which applies to business colleagues as well as to social relationships.

- Finally, a word of warning. Deliberate mirroring can only help you when the non-verbal signal is a positive or constructive one. For example, when your boss leans back in his chair, puts his hands on his head and shows as clearly as he can that he's the one with the authority, copying his behaviour will just get up his nose. Similarly, when your bank manager's body language is saying all too clearly that she's not impressed with your business plan you won't change her mind by mirroring her movements and expressions.

PLAYING IT COOL

As well as speaking and understanding the body language of friendship, there are times when you have to deal with its opposite. Few of us are brave (or rude) enough to tell someone to their face that we don't like them or want to be left alone. Equally, we can avoid time-wasting and possible embarrassment by recognising when an encounter is going nowhere without waiting to be told.

Top turn-offs
A study carried out in the USA by Dr Gerald Clore and his colleagues led to the devising of a list of the kinds of behaviour which their subjects interpreted as the main signs of dislike.

- frowning
- low levels of eye contact
- moving away
- yawning
- sneering
- picking your teeth
- shaking your head
- cleaning your fingernails

All these are pretty unmistakable and you would very likely receive the intended message loud and clear. When the other person's behaviour is less overt, you may feel uncomfortable without being sure of the reason. Once again, what's known as 'body pointing' can be literally a signpost to their true feelings. We saw earlier how the position of feet can indicate which way someone's thoughts are going – and if your companion has positioned his or hers facing out past you, you can assume a quick getaway might be welcome. A similar message can come across from a sitting position too – leaning away or legs crossed away from you are signs of emotional retreat. Incidentally, when this happens, you should not always take it personally. Your companion may have something on their mind that has nothing to do with your charm or lack of it – so don't go getting depressed or assume you're a complete social failure. Only if this kind of thing happens every time you try to impress someone should you consider seeking counselling.

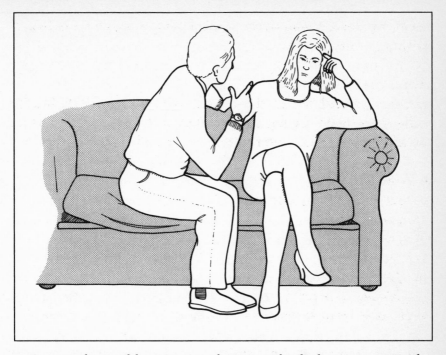

Crossing legs and leaning away from an individual are sure signs of emotional retreat.

While you may sometimes be on the receiving end of cold behaviour like this, you will probably also want to use it yourself on occasion. When you're desperate to escape from someone but unwilling to be direct about it, you could opt for complete withdrawal of your attention. This is harder than it sounds, because good manners and politeness have been drilled into most of us with great effect. Nevertheless, you have to steel yourself to stop giving normal social rewards: don't make any of the usual encouraging remarks and noises such as, 'Really?', 'I know what you mean', or even nod in synthetic agreement. Just as important, avoid looking at the other person's face and stop making eye contact. Few people will persist in the face of such obvious signs of lack of interest, and will usually find someone else to target. Women may have to try particularly hard to carry out this manoeuvre because supportive and sympathetic behaviour often comes more naturally to them than it does to men. What's more, as we've seen already, men in general are less sensitive to subtle body language, so you may have to be quite blatant to make your lack of interest crystal clear to the oblivious type.

PUTTING UP BARRIERS

We saw in chapter 4 how you can use physical barriers such as desks to intimidate others and warn them against getting too close. You can achieve a similar effect by making use of less tangible but equally understandable symbolic barriers. The reverse is also true, of course, in that you can demonstrate openness and accessibility to others by *avoiding* defensive postures – you probably use both methods all the time.

Most experts define barriers as specific ways of positioning your arms or legs, or both, which will have negative connotations of some kind. A few will go so far as to ascribe minutely different meanings according to the exact position of the arms, hands, thumbs and so on.

Do you use these defence mechanisms?

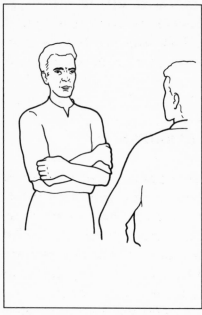

Folding your arms

Whether you know it or not, you're most likely to do this when you're feeling insecure or unsure of yourself, especially when you're with people you don't know very well. When you're feeling threatened, you may well clench your fists at the same time, or grip your arms when you're in a negative frame of mind. However, as so often with body language, this isn't foolproof, so don't be too quick to jump to conclusions.

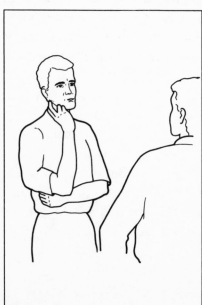

Arm across your body

This is a slightly more subtle version of folded arms, when you hold one elbow with the other hand. It looks more natural, but is still a sign of defensiveness. Insecure people make 'excuses' for putting their arms across their body, such as checking cuff links or looking at their watch.

119

Two-handed grip

You can sometimes use an innocent-looking object – such as a drink glass, handbag or document case – as a means of self-protection by holding it in front of you with both hands. You may think this will disguise your nervousness but you're probably wrong in that most people will still read the signal, albeit unconsciously.

Holding a cigarette

One very strong deterrent against an invasion of your space is the hot, glowing tip of a lighted cigarette which threatens to singe anyone who gets too close. Blowing smoke directly into someone's face is an equally unsubtle sign of rejection. But these days, just smoking a cigarette at all may be sufficient to keep other people well away from you.

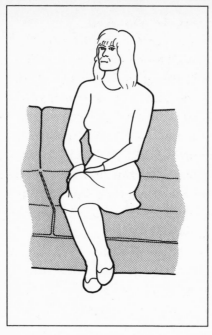

Crossing your legs

Although you may often do this when you're feeling negative or under threat, it is less easy for others to interpret accurately. Women are often taught that it's a 'ladylike' way to sit, or may have other objectives in mind, such as looking sexy (for more on this, see chapter 7).

Taking a stand

It's quite possible to stand with both your arms and legs crossed – and it's what most of us do when we're in a group of strangers. The others are likely to be doing the same thing, and you'll know the group is warming up as people start to unravel their crossed-up limbs!

It is very difficult for most people to avoid these defensive manoeuvres even when they want to. Crossing your arms or protecting your body with one arm is such an instinctive reaction when you're ill at ease that you'll probably find you've done it as soon as you stop thinking about not doing it. It's further complicated because many people actually fold their arms when they're cold, and women often find it's simply comfortable to do it when they're standing. In both these instances, you will need to use other criteria besides folded arms to get an accurate assessment of someone's true feelings.

It's worth remembering that you will come across as friendly and receptive to other people if you adopt an open posture, and it may even help to ease your own tension. Studies have shown that audiences at lectures felt much more friendly towards the speaker and took in more of his message when they sat in a relaxed and open position. In other words, a negative and defensive posture actually reinforces those feelings.

DON'T BE SHY

For a shy person, the prospect of starting up a conversation with a complete stranger is terrifying. Learning how to use body language can't solve this problem for you overnight, but it may help you to cope better in social situations. Most shy people are fearful of meeting new people because they are conscious they are being assessed and feel sure that they won't make a good impression. Sadly, this is to some extent a self-fulfilling prophecy. If you concentrate on your own feelings and worry about how you are coming across, you won't respond positively to the other person's advances and they will assume you're not interested or are unfriendly. As we saw above, avoiding eye contact, defensive postures and smiling rarely, are what people do when they're trying to avoid or escape the person they're talking to, and other people may not guess that you are behaving in this way because you're shy. Even if you're terrified underneath, 'acting' friendly by responding with positive body language will help others to think that you're interested in them and so they'll be more inclined to like you. The first time you manage to do it successfully will give you such a kick that hopefully it will be easier next time round. That's not to say, of course, that dealing with shyness is a simple matter. For some people, it is simply a part of their personality and will always be present to some degree. Understanding body language techniques may help a shy person to behave like someone who does not experience these feelings in social situations. In this way, others are encouraged to react more positively towards them so that meeting strangers becomes less of an ordeal.

CHAPTER 7

The secrets of sex appeal

———

'What on earth does he see in her?'
'She'd never look at someone like me.'
'How can such a plain man be so sexy?'

Just what is it that makes one person sexually attractive to you while another leaves you cold? And why does one person attract admirers by the dozen while another is perpetually left out? There are no simple answers to any of these questions and it's probably just as well. If we all agreed on what makes someone desirable, those without the necessary qualities would be doomed to lifelong loneliness and celibacy. While looks and that indefinable chemistry between two people may be vital factors in some relationships, others grow more slowly and don't depend on an initial spark of attraction. You may know someone for years as a colleague or friend before reaching the point where sex comes into your feelings for one another. Or you may believe in love at first sight, or have experienced what the French call a *coup de foudre* where the attraction is instant and total. It's fair to say that while there is always an individual element – a feeling about the other person that is unique to you – there are also some common factors that apply to most people.

WHO TURNS YOU ON?

- **Who are your favourite sexual fantasy figures?**
  Most of us could draw up a short list of around half a dozen

people we'd like to be alone on a desert island with, even if we are already in a happy relationship. It doesn't matter whether it includes your doctor, the next-door neighbour, a national newsreader or the singer in your favourite pop group. The point is that there is something about these individuals that appeals to you, even though you may hardly know them or have never met them at all.

- **What, if anything, do they have in common?**
  At first the answer may seem to be 'nothing much', but often closer consideration will reveal that they all have sexy eyes, narrow hips, smiling mouths, artistic talent, sparkling wit or whatever.

- **Is it how they look or something else which attracts you?**
  There have been many surveys suggesting that men are more likely to be attracted to a woman because of the way she looks. Women, while by no means immune to physical charms, usually put other qualities such as kindness or a sense of humour high on their list of desirable qualities in their ideal man. With fantasy figures you don't have to concern yourself with what the person is really like – provided they have sex appeal for you, you can ascribe any other qualities you like to them regardless of reality.

- **How similar are they to your current or past real-life partner(s)?**
  Research shows that in real life, we are most likely to choose partners who resemble ourselves. While you might fantasise over the drop-dead gorgeous film star, you will probably be content with someone more ordinary-looking if you don't rate your own physical charms that highly. The same is true when it comes to other factors like education, social class, religion and politics in that we're more likely to opt for someone similar to rather than wildly different from ourselves.

- **Do friends share your fantasy or wonder at your strange taste?**

We've all come across examples of the 'What on earth does she see in him?' couples who nevertheless seem delighted with one another. Just who you find attractive, and why, has its roots in your own personal psychology, even though external factors may play a part. Pop music moguls consciously exploit variations in taste when putting together or promoting new acts – most bands feature a selection of stereotypes to appeal as widely as possible, so there'll be 'the Rebel', 'the Quiet One', 'the Intelligent One', 'the Clown', and so on. It worked with the Beatles, the Stones and, even more obviously, with the Monkees, and works just as effectively today – think of Take That and Blur.

- **How would you feel if fantasy became reality?**
  It's one thing to dream over the image you've created, but many people would balk if offered the chance of starting a real relationship with their fantasy figure. Most of us have the sense to realise that we wouldn't necessarily find the real person as appealing as the illusion, and that while a successful relationship may start with mutual physical attraction, it needs more than that to survive.

IT'S IN YOUR GENES

While economic and social changes, in some Western societies at least, are having their effects on the relations between men and women, they are not powerful enough to overcome evolutionary biology completely. By this definition of what attractiveness means, the odds favour sexy-looking women and socially dominant men.

Before you protest that your approach is nowhere near so crude, look at what sex is about from an evolutionary point of view.

Older men, younger women
With some exceptions, women pair off with men who are older than them. Many people think that this is because girls mature earlier than boys, and it's true that girls reach sexual maturity about two years ahead of their male counterparts. By the time they all reach adulthood, and begin choosing partners, however, this effect has largely worn off. The real reason for the age discrepancy is because a woman's prime suit – her physical beauty – peaks in her late teens or early twenties, whereas a man's social power, which is his strongest suit, continues to increase into his thirties and beyond.

The biological significance of beauty in a woman is the role it plays in determining her potential capacity as a mother. Youth is important because a woman's eggs are present in her body from birth, and susceptible to damage from radiation, viruses and chemical poisoning. As a woman gets older, her chances of having 100 per cent healthy offspring decrease, so evolution has ensured that she is most strongly attractive to men in her teens and twenties when she is in prime breeding condition. The position is different with men in that their stud value does not decline with age while their ability to display social accomplishment increases.

Successful men in recent history, such as Lloyd George, Charlie Chaplin, Paul Getty, Bertrand Russell and John F. Kennedy had little difficulty in winning younger partners because their 'breeding quality' was well recognised. It's not wealth as such that matters, but what that wealth says about their ability to compete.

Measuring motherhood potential
The most crucial aspects of a woman's appearance from this perspective are those which mark her out specifically as female. To state the obvious, physical attraction is based in the differences between the sexes. The parts of the body which

most encapsulate these differences are the focuses of attraction and arousal, and the more exaggerated they are, within reason, the sexier. Make-up and beauty treatments are designed to emphasise the ways in which a woman's face is different from a man's – fuller lips, bigger eyes, finer eyebrows, softer complexion, absence of facial hair and so on.

Large breasts are attractive unless they are so big that they droop, which is seen as a sign of old age. Narrow waists and rounded hips are appealing because men don't have them. The distinctive way a woman walks (which is seen in an extreme form in the so-called 'Monroe wiggle') results from the fact that the female pelvis is shaped for childbirth as much as for walking.

Many of these signals are biological in origin. Large breasts and shapely hips imply that a woman is good child-bearing material, while a narrow waist indicates that she is not already pregnant. These basic facts are reflected in the fact that most men prefer the traditional Playboy or 'page three' images of women to the ultra-thin fashion model figures that women themselves often aspire to. Interestingly, some other features have social rather than biological origins – for example, long hair and fingernails are seen as sexy in women, even though men could have either or both if they chose. They have become female signals because they are inappropriate to traditional male work, where they would be impractical or even dangerous.

Sizing up the men
Although women take a wider view when assessing the attractiveness of men, surveys have shown some shared preferences as far as male bodies are concerned. It's hardly surprising perhaps that the muscular Schwarzenegger-style physique – all big chest, bulging biceps and powerful shoulders – seldom impresses women. Only around one per cent admit to being sexually

aroused by looking at such men. The majority prefer men of more modest proportions, and would rather see them dressed than naked. Reassuringly for men, perhaps, they also deny being obsessed with penis size. What does turn many women on, apparently, is the sight of a man's bottom, especially if it is a small, firm one set off in tight trousers or jeans. As many as thirty per cent of women agree that small buttocks are the feature they find most visually exciting. Further down the popularity lists comes tallness, slimness (that is, a flat tummy), and a certain look in the eye!

These preferences can be explained in purely biological terms too. Viewed from behind, a small bottom is the easiest way of distinguishing a man from a woman. The pelvis is the part of the skeleton which differs most according to sex, and for reasons that are vital to reproduction. Big muscles are attractive up to a point, but if a man's chest bulges too much, it becomes rounded and starts to look too much like a woman's breasts.

Social learning plays its part in these preferences too. Women tend to regard muscle-bound men as thick-headed narcissists who are unlikely to have the necessary qualities to achieve dominant status in sophisticated human society. And women may prefer to see a man dressed rather than naked because clothes are an important clue to status. Being tall, as we've already seen in chapter 5, appears to make a man more likely to be successful in career terms and, in any case, many women feel self-conscious if their partner is shorter than them as they are worried others will think they look ridiculous together.

THE PERFECT FACE

Faces are very important when it comes to sex appeal. Conventional prettiness actually seems to come down to two basic elements: symmetry and an absence of blemishes. This rather dull conclusion was first demonstrated in the last century by Sir Francis Galton, using a technique of his own invention called composite portraiture. He superimposed several people's faces on to a photographic plate to produce a single image. Features common to most of the faces were retained, while bumps, blotches and any peculiarities were eliminated. The result, according to Galton, was 'a very striking face, thoroughly ideal and artistic, and singularly beautiful'. It would seem that the face we're most likely to regard as attractive is relatively bland: the nose neither too long nor too short, the eyes neither too close together nor too far apart, and so on. Add to these basics a smooth complexion, clear whites to the eyes and good teeth (seen when their owner smiles) and we have a face that will probably be called beautiful. Looking beyond the aesthetics to an evolutionary explanation, it is clear that an unblemished face signifies good health and therefore good breeding material. Since Galton's averaging of faces was done for men and women separately, there are really two average faces – one male and one female. Since we find members of the opposite sex attractive because of the differences between them and us, a face in which these points of difference are slightly exaggerated has more appeal. Just as make-up is designed to highlight the female differences, a woman with a truly feminine face – large eyes, narrow eyebrows, soft complexion and so on – tends to be seen as pretty. By the same token, men with rugged, masculine looks – strong jaw, bushy eyebrows and the like – are said to be handsome.

But why do women's faces differ from men's in the way that they do? Apparently women have evolved in such a way as to mirror the appealing signals used by the human baby to trigger its parents' protective instincts. Children's eyes are larger in relation to their head size than adults', and the same is true of women compared with men. Women can't see better than men

– if anything, the reverse is the case. Their big eyes are designed to attract men and win support from them. The message is: 'I'm a baby, look after me.' The same applies to other female features such as a small chin, soft complexion, hairlessness, large lips and a generally rounded look. Evolution has determined that women should imitate the looks and gestures of children to encourage men to give them love. The swarthy, bristly male face is better designed for frightening enemies and rivals.

As always, there are natural limits on these developments. A completely helpless and childlike woman is unlikely to be an effective mother. And when men are past the age of fighting tigers and competing successfully, they lose their hair and develop rounded stomachs in the instinctive hope that some woman will mother them. Men are more prone than women to go into a 'second childhood' because they are still capable of fathering children in their later years and can therefore benefit genetically from such a strategy, whereas women who are past the menopause cannot.

WHEN LOVE ISN'T BLIND . . .

Until you get to know someone, all you have to go on is the way they look. We all screen strangers on the basis of their physical attractiveness, and mentally divide them into possibles and unsuitables. There have been several studies which reveal that physical cues are given priority when we make snap judgements about other people, and this is especially true when men are evaluating women. For example, one study showed that male drivers were more likely to stop for a female hitchhiker when her breasts had been padded to accentuate their size.

When it comes to picking a potential partner, we are just as likely to reject someone who's too good-looking as we are someone who's too plain. We learn to judge our own level of attractiveness and avoid aiming too high for fear of being rejected. Studies in which men and women were asked to choose someone they'd like to meet from a selection of photos found that most people were fairly realistic in selecting others similar in attractiveness to themselves. Couples who are already in a relationship are also usually similarly matched in this respect. One research team looked at couples in theatre and cinema bars and lobbies and rated each individual on a scale of one to five in attractiveness. They found that 85 per cent of couples were within one point of each other. Those pairs where the gap was wider were less likely to hold hands or kiss, suggesting either that they were not romantically involved or that their relationship was faltering.

Choosing someone who is roughly your equal when it comes to attractiveness is one example of what's called 'assortive mating'. Your relationship is more likely to last if you choose a partner who is similar in other important respects, including age, height, geographical origin, religion, politics, intelligence and interests. It seems there is little evidence to justify the belief that opposites attract, except with respect to the attributes on which the two genders traditionally differ – for example, independent men like dependent women, and vice versa.

SEXUAL SIGNALLING

When we meet someone we find attractive, knowing that many of our responses are programmed into our genes makes not the slightest difference. All we know is that here is someone appealing – and we want to get that person to show a reciprocal interest. We try to signal our own attraction, but usually in such a way that we won't be embarrassed if we don't get the response we're hoping for. So while our mouths are saying quite ordinary, even banal things, a separate 'conversation' is being conducted through body language. In part, this will be similar to the signals we use when we simply want to be friendly – making eye contact, smiling, taking up an 'open' body posture and so on – but we'll probably throw some specifically flirtatious signals into the mix as well. Many people do this quite unconsciously, and making a deliberate effort to learn and adopt these techniques can be counter-productive. Being subtle is a lot more effective and less likely to frighten your intended than obvious vampishness. Nevertheless, it is interesting to analyse the ways men and women play the chasing game.

Two can play . . .
Both sexes can make use of certain signs of attraction and encouragement, although as with most aspects of body language, women generally use it more and understand it better than most men.

- Faced with someone they find sexually attractive, both a man and a woman will unconsciously tighten their muscles, standing straight, drawing in their stomach, pulling their shoulders back and so on. Interestingly, this tightening can also be seen in muscles over which you have no control – your face looks less puffy and any sagging around your eyes decreases!
- As we saw earlier, dilated pupils are a possible sign of arousal and likely to be noted as such, albeit subconsciously, even by people who are not generally good at understanding subtle signals.
- Unconscious preening is something both sexes do – patting or smoothing their hair, adjusting their clothes or brushing off imaginary specks.
- When standing or sitting together, a couple will 'point' their bodies towards each other. Standing face to face, they'll point

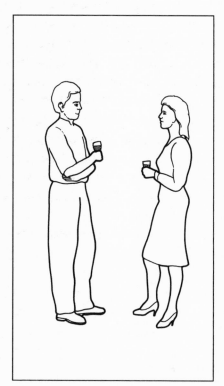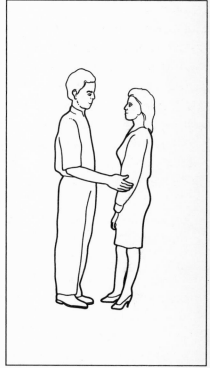

At first, two people who find each other sexually attractive will stand tall and face each other, feet pointing towards each other. As they become more comfortable, they may begin to touch each other tentatively.

137

their feet directly towards each other, making it more difficult for anyone else to break into their tête-à-tête. When seated, they may shift so as to face towards the other person, again effectively shutting out anyone who might try to intrude.

- Although not strictly in the realms of body language, pretending to teach one another some physical activity such as darts or a dance step has great possibilities when it comes to flirtation. It allows you to get close and touch one another and often leads to a lot of joking and giggling. Neither of you need admit that you're not really interested in the teaching or the learning, although you both know it perfectly well.

Games she plays

There's an old saying that 'a man chases a woman until she catches him', which although it sounds rather sexist to our ears, still contains an element of truth. On the surface at least, men still make the running and learn to be more direct about their intentions, while most women rely on more subtle ways of conveying their interest.

- Women who are genuinely shy with the opposite sex will often catch a man's eye then turn away and blush. Even when they make eye contact quite deliberately then look away, this is likely to be interpreted in the same way – that is, as an invitation to chase.

- A variation on this theme is what the tabloid newspapers used to refer to as the 'Shy Di' look, referring to the habit the Princess of Wales has of looking up into someone's face through her eyelashes while keeping her head lowered and on one side. It is flirtatious because it arouses a protective feeling in many men – although of course it does help to have eyes as large and eyelashes as long as Diana's.

138

The 'Shy Di' look.

- Hair is a potent sexual symbol as we've seen, so playing with it or tossing it back – even when it's actually too short for this to have much real effect – is a popular ploy.
- Sitting down offers a variety of options for signalling sexual interest. Crossing one leg over the other at the knee and pressing the calves together keeps the leg muscles taut, implying that the woman is sexually alert. As we've seen, high muscle tone is one of the ways our bodies prepare for sexual activity.
- Allowing one shoe to dangle and moving your foot slowly in and out of it is one way a woman shows she is relaxed – it may be seen as a prelude to undressing and has obvious symbolic significance. The 'come-on' is further reinforced if a woman sits with one leg folded under her and the other knee pointing towards the man of her choice.

139

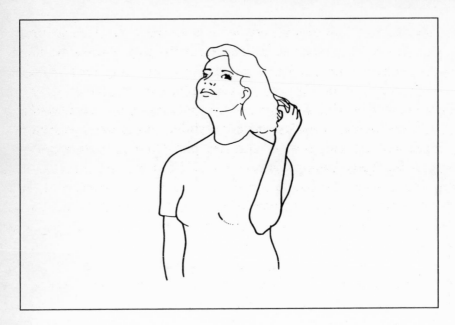

Preening

Body pointing and shoe dangling.

- Standing with one hand resting on her hip is a classic pose for a woman who wants to look sexually inviting – film stars in the thirties and forties went in for it in a big way. The message is a provocative, challenging one which may be translated as: 'Here I am – *are you man enough to come and take me?*' It can look a little unsubtle, and is perhaps best reserved for those men who are particularly dense about reading body language.

'Here I am.'

- You may be surprised to learn that a woman who reveals the inside of her wrists by pushing up long sleeves and turning them towards a man is indicating her interest in him. Exposing the soft skin in this area and showing the palms of her hand while speaking is something many women do naturally in this situation.

Games he plays
Men have a smaller repertoire of signals and they tend to be a lot less subtle.

● When he's standing, a man may move his legs further apart and stick his thumbs into his belt or waistband. This has the effect of leaving his fingers pointing down towards his crotch, so may be avoided by men who don't want to appear too blatantly macho or sexually aggressive.

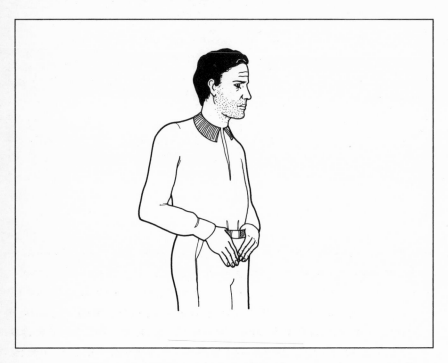

'Here are my credentials.'

● A similar but less crude message can be conveyed by a man putting his hand into a pocket in his jacket or trousers. The woman can't then see which way his hand is pointing, but the signal is there none the less.

- A further variation on this theme is standing with hands on hips – another crotch display, but one to be used with caution as it can come across as rather camp, especially if only one hand is used and the wrist is turned under in an effeminate manner.

Hands on hips.

- When sitting down, some men will spread their legs as a means of advertising their wares to a woman who interests them. She may not find this especially appealing, but at least the signal is difficult to miss!

A WOLF IN SHEEP'S CLOTHING?

We've already looked in chapter 2 at the effect clothes have in forming other people's first impressions of you. The very first thing a potential partner is going to notice about you is your appearance, so it's worth giving some thought to this. It's true that in some circumstances, such as a job interview, the most important thing is to dress in a way that's appropriate. Even on the social front the same can apply: a man wearing a suit on the beach or a woman arriving at a formal dinner party in Lycra shorts would make a somewhat eccentric impression.

But you want your appearance to reflect your personality, so don't be afraid to take the lead and assert your individuality. The person who is over-concerned with wearing the correct, socially acceptable uniform on all occasions may just come across as a boring conformist.

It has been the case throughout history that the most socially powerful people suffer fewest restraints when it comes to clothes and grooming. In medieval times, only a knight was permitted to wear a tunic so short that the lines of his buttocks were revealed. In the modern British navy, an officer may grow a beard, but an ordinary sailor requires special permission to do so. In the same way, film and pop stars who are rich and famous have the freedom to appear unconventional, whereas a civil servant or a bank clerk must keep a lower profile and conform to certain standards laid down by others. Being an individualist when it comes to style doesn't just mean being outrageous. What you're aiming for is to make your appearance an extension of your personality. 'Be yourself' is a good guideline for clothes and self-presentation in general as well as for your behaviour. It is counter-productive to tart yourself up in a seductive way if you are really a shy or sexually restrained person. You will simply attract the wrong kind of attention and end up being labelled as a tease. By the same token, you are unlikely to attract sexy, adventurous people by wearing drab, passion-killing clothes.

You may feel that you should be able to dress in any way you like without concerning yourself with other people's reactions, but you have to live in the real world. Whether you like it or not, your appearance will influence the way others react to you, and you make life difficult for yourself if you don't project the appropriate message. Some men are actually aware that a woman who chooses a low-cut, body hugging dress or a clinging mini-skirt is not necessarily advertising her nympho-maniac tendencies. She may just be wearing the latest fashion item or an outfit she happens to like. Nevertheless, the majority probably won't think this way, and will assume that she is sexually available. Men have less scope to flaunt their sexuality through their clothes. Few women these days are impressed by the shirt open to the navel to reveal a muscular, hairy chest – with or without a gold medallion. Because women use other criteria besides physique when summing up a man, his style of dress may convey more complex messages. Obviously expen-sive, well-cut and well-fitting clothes may indicate a man's financial and social status which is far more significant than the size of his muscles. Men in positions of authority have never had trouble attracting women and many of them were (and are) not film-star material. Aristotle Onassis, for instance, would hardly have relied on his looks to attract Maria Callas or Jackie Kennedy, but then, as Henry Kissinger, another rather plain man put it, 'Power is the ultimate aphrodisiac.'

There's no reason why you shouldn't opt for an unusual or even bizarre style, but it could be revealing to reflect for a moment on what message you are conveying. A man who favours a 'Hell's Angel' look is going to attract a different kind of woman from the Armani-suit brigade, for example. Whatever you choose, the most important thing is that you feel happy and comfortable. Even if you suspect your outfit might be wrong for the occasion, don't let it show. If you wear your clothes with confidence and panache – to the manner born – you can get away with virtually anything. Aim to make sure your personality dominates your clothes rather than the other way round, and the world will get the message loud and clear.

145

WHAT YOUR HAIR SAYS

Everyone needs to wash and comb their hair and have it in some kind of style. Even men these days use conditioners and will even purchase products to improve the appearance of their skin. Most women feel they look better wearing make-up and, well-applied, it usually produces a favourable reaction from other people too. The art of this kind of grooming consists of looking as if you haven't tried – as though your appearance is natural and not the result of hours spent titivating in front of the mirror. Women don't usually go for men who seem more interested in their own appearance than that of their partner, while a woman who is so 'done up' as to appear untouchable isn't appealing either. Most men prefer a woman who looks as if she could be touched (and possibly kissed) without major structural damage.

While it's still true that long hair on women is regarded as sexy and on men as a sign of non-conformity, reactions are probably less stereotyped than they used to be. Blondes don't have to be dumb, redheads hot-tempered or brunettes sultry, and it's not only tall, dark men who are regarded as handsome. Styles, especially for women, can emphasise the image created by other aspects of their appearance. A short neat cap of shining hair may say 'efficient' or 'authoritative' on a woman wearing a business suit, while a tousled, just-fallen-out-of-bed style reinforces the effect of a sexy outfit. Women can (and do) have a lot of fun changing the colour and style of their hair to alter their image, either temporarily or permanently. Men again have fewer options in terms of style and colour and most simply adapt the length to the current norm or the demands of their workplace. Beards and moustaches on the other hand, can be grown or abolished, trimmed carefully or allowed to straggle. An unkempt beard may fit the image of a painter or university

146

researcher, while a neatly maintained one might be a gesture of minor rebellion in a businessman. How women react to facial hair is an individual matter – some like it, some hate it, but relatively few are neutral. And, just to be difficult, a woman may dislike beards in general while feeling that one just happens to suit her particular Mr Right.

THE SWEET SMELL OF SUCCESS

Smell is often treated as the Cinderella of the senses, in that we take less conscious notice of what our nose tells us than we do of what we see, hear, touch and taste. Yet it has a powerful and long-lasting effect on us, and can affect our mood and responses in dramatic ways. The well-known wine writer Jane MacQuitty tells a story about visiting her mother one day and immediately recognising the perfume she was wearing. 'It reminds me of the time you used to come and kiss me goodnight when you and Father were going out.' Her mother was astonished because the perfume, Rêve d'Or, had been discontinued, but she had recently found an old bottle in the attic and put it on for the first time in twenty years.

Smells are deeply embedded in our memory in this way because they are processed by ancient parts of the brain closely connected with the memory circuits. This area of the brain, known as the limbic system, is also concerned with emotion and sexuality, which explains why smells not only evoke deep-seated feelings but also powerful sensations of attraction and revulsion.

Smell is a fundamental sense not just in terms of its early evolution, but also because it involves sampling actual molecules from the environment. This is why it's not surprising that the feelings of pleasantness or unpleasantness evoked by smells are particularly direct and powerful.

Our capacity for smell is often underestimated. It is true that other animals are more sensitive than humans – dogs, for example, have twenty times as many smell receptors in their noses. But although the evolution of primates like us has favoured the development of sight and hearing, our capacity for smell remains quite remarkable. You could still detect the smell of a single molecule of mercaptan (a chemical produced by skunks and rotten meat) when it was mixed with 50 trillion molecules of air, for instance. Wine connoisseurs, perfumers and gourmets make the most of an ability to smell which has simply been overshadowed by newer, more informative senses, but is still there in the deeper recesses of the mind. We may not consciously attend to smells for much of the time, but they influence us all the same. This fact is being increasingly exploited in all manner of ways – soothing smells are fed into the air conditioning in offices and underground train systems, newly baked bread odours are wafted out of the entrances to supermarkets and some secondhand car dealers spray their vehicles with a chemically produced 'new car' aerosol. You may have heard that people showing potential buyers around their home sometimes leave a few coffee beans under a low grill to give off a welcoming scent of fresh coffee.

Communicating by smell

Our sense of smell is important to us from the moment we are born and is more significant to a newborn baby than the sense of sight. Studies have shown babies recognise their mothers by her smell well before they are able to pick out her face from that of other adults. Later, the ability to distinguish smells plays an important role in social and sexual communication, even though we are often not consciously aware that it is happening at all.

After puberty, our bodies begin to produce hormone-like chemicals called pheromones which give off a distinctive smell.

148

They are emitted from the apocrine glands, which are concentrated in the underarm and genital areas, where body hair
helps to trap and propagate them. Body odours are the result
not just of sweating when we've been exerting ourselves, but
also of our apocrine glands going into action in response to
emotions such as excitement and fear. Men have more and
larger apocrine glands than women and there are variations
between people of different ethnic origins too. Black people
have more than Caucasians who, in turn, have more than
Orientals. It is said that the air-freshener aerosol was originally
invented by the Japanese to get rid of the smell left behind by
visiting Westerners.

Individuals also vary in that each of us produces our own
unique smell. Marilyn Monroe attracted most people who came
near her and, according to Norman Mailer, assistants in dress
shops would claim 'She has a smell' – presumably a pleasant
one. The writer H. G. Wells had surprising success with women
considering his lack of obvious physical attractions, but one of
his mistresses explained the secret of his desirability: 'He smells
of honey,' she said. Family members can recognise one another
by smell, and it's interesting that the only individuals who share
the same odour are identical twins – even trained sniffer dogs
are confused by them.

One of the earliest indications that humans communicate
through pheromones was the discovery that women who live or
work closely together tend to have their periods at the same
time – a phenomenon known as 'menstrual synchrony'. The
only feasible explanation of this seems to be pheromonal, and
researchers at the University of Pittsburgh suggest that women
respond to the one among them who has the greatest output of
male hormone during menstruation by gradually synchronising
their cycle with hers.

Studies have shown that while women are good at detecting
male pheromones, especially at the time of ovulation, men are

less reliable in this respect, though some are more sensitive than others. Interestingly, research has discovered that women release a pheromone called copulin in their vaginal secretions which peaks during ovulation. Copulin is one of the so-called 'attractant' pheromones, so presumably it makes a woman more desirable at the time in her cycle when she is also most fertile. When she is taking the contraceptive pill, a woman secretes less copulin, which raises interesting questions about what effect this may have on her sex life. As well as 'attractant' pheromones, men release others which have a 'priming' effect: that is they speed up ovulation and may also make a woman more sexually receptive.

An 'attractant' pheromone called androstenol is secreted by men in their sweat and urine which women can detect at lower concentrations than men, especially when they are ovulating. Farmers use androstenol (under the brand name Boarmate) to make female pigs more sexually receptive, and you can also buy it in sex shops, although its effect on human, as opposed to pig, females is uncertain. In its natural state, most people think androstenol smells like musk, although some associate it more with sandalwood; however, contact with air and bacteria transform it into androsterone, which smells more like urine.

Various interesting experiments have been conducted to see whether women are actually turned on by the smell of male pheromones. One found that given a choice of six telephone booths, women were more likely to use the one which had been sprayed with androstenol. A similar study showed the same effect with seats in a dentist's waiting room – women were more likely to sit in the treated seats while men tended to avoid them. Spraying androstenol into the air before showing a mixed group a series of photos of both men and women resulted in the people in the photos being rated as warmer and more sexually attractive by both sexes, but especially by the opposite sex.

Apparently, we can all tell the difference between the smell of a man and that of a woman. The experiment which demonstrated this involved the unfortunate participants sniffing T-shirts which had been impregnated with the underarm odours of their wearers. Most people (including other women) preferred the smell of women, which was described as sweeter.

All this 'underground' signalling can be seen as a kind of socio-biological battle of the sexes. From this perspective, men can be said to have an interest in producing pheromones that will make women more sexually receptive and fertile, and at the same time scare off potential male rivals. Women need to attract men, but without driving them crazy or out of control. So although androstenol production has obvious sexual and evolutionary advantages for men, women's production of pheromones is something of a balancing act. Having enhanced sensory awareness around ovulation time may help them to pick the right partner, yet they might be better off if the signals transmitted by copulins could be minimised.

Even before scientists began to study and reveal the secrets of pheromones, people still behaved as though they already knew all about them. Many cultures have scent rituals – some Mediterranean dances involve young men rubbing handkerchiefs under their armpits and waving them in front of their female partners. Ironically, in modern western society we go to great lengths to remove or cover up these powerful natural secretions. We wash ourselves constantly and replace or disguise our natural smells with all manner of artificial fragrances which probably do far less to attract the opposite sex.

What your perfume says . . .
We may think we choose perfume because we like the smell or think it will enhance our attractiveness, but in practice our choice is often heavily influenced by marketing. The makers of fragrances and toiletries for both men and women spend millions of pounds trying to persuade us to buy one brand rather

151

than another. Research shows that while perfumers make subtle distinctions between perfumes, assigning them to numerous categories, most buyers only discriminate much more broadly. The main distinctions we recognise are sweet (or floral) and non-sweet (or dry). Beyond that, it seems, we choose more on the basis of image than smell. When people were asked to smell well-known perfumes such as Opium, Shalimar, Poison and Miss Dior without knowing what they were, they rated the first three as being very different from one another. But when they knew what they were smelling, they thought Opium, Poison and Shalimar similar, and Miss Dior quite different. In fact Opium and Miss Dior are quite alike. It seems that the rich, sensual image associated with the first three has more to do with the packaging and promotion than with how they actually smell.

BE ON YOUR GUARD

Flirting and getting to know someone you find attractive almost inevitably involves some degree of game-playing. Each of you is trying to put yourself across as well as possible and at the same time to gauge the other person's response. You won't always be as direct in this situation as you would with a colleague or an old friend and there's often a lot of attempted manipulation on both sides. This doesn't matter at all, and can be enormous fun, provided both of you know you are playing and operate by the same unspoken rules. The problems can start when you meet someone whose agenda is different from yours, especially if they are skilled at concealing what they're really up to. If you're genuinely interested in the possibility of a relationship, you need to be able to recognise someone who just wants to add another name to his or her list of conquests. Unfortunately, there's no guaranteed way to spot a fake, but you may be able to pick up on one or two suspicious behaviours.

Warning signs

- Is there a perceptible gap between the initial impression you got from the person's appearance and the image they're now putting across? It could be because they are overdoing the effort to please you rather than revealing anything of their true self.
- Try and get an overall picture of their body language. Is their friendly smile contradicted by a tense posture or an anxiously tapping foot?
- Are they over-reacting by laughing excessively at your jokes or agreeing rather too warmly with everything you say?
- Watch their gaze – does it convey a real interest in what you're saying or does it feel rather too intense?
- Is their sexual signalling a bit too overt for comfort? Of course you want to know that they find you attractive, but you might wonder about someone who sets a pace that's too fast for you.
- Does their tone of voice seem very different from yours, or their conversation seem to be following a pre-determined chat-up line rather than responding to what you're saying?
- Are their pupils dilated? As we've seen this is a sign of arousal and often of sexual interest, so be suspicious of anyone who's acting interested without enlarged pupils.

All of these things could have innocent explanations. Some people are just not very good at getting it right when they meet someone they find attractive. All the same, it's worth making a mental note of your reaction even if you decide to give them the benefit of the doubt for the time being. Make up your mind once you've spent a bit longer together and have more to go on.

Overt sexual signalling.

PLAYING HARD TO GET

In some respects, this is the opposite of the person who wants to captivate everyone they meet, regardless of whether they are genuinely interested in them as individuals. It may be a risky game to play, but experiments have shown that it can sometimes be very successful. Basically, the idea is that when you first meet someone who attracts you, you deliberately avoid showing it and withhold all the signs that indicate your interest. So you don't smile or make eye contact very much, and maintain a defensive or even hostile posture and are sparing with your nods of encouragement. The skill lies in going just far enough to disturb or unbalance the other person without frightening them off altogether. Then, when you judge the

154

time is right, you change your tune and become much warmer and more receptive.

There are various explanations of why people respond to this cold and hot treatment. One is that by only gradually responding, you prove that you are revealing a genuine liking for the other person as you get to know them, and that this isn't the way you treat just anyone. Some people feel they have enough close friends and lovers already and have no desire to extend their social circle indiscriminately, and so they get into the habit of erecting barriers which newcomers can't penetrate. An alternative theory is that being rude or indifferent when you first meet someone temporarily lowers their self-esteem, so they are much more susceptible when you eventually show your charming side.

It's as well to recognise when you've been on the receiving end of such treatment. It might seem manipulative, but if it's done because someone is attracted to you and keen that you should reciprocate, you may be flattered rather than offended. Whether you choose to try the technique yourself depends on your confidence in your ability to judge the situation finely so that the object of your interest isn't driven away before you have the chance to reveal your true feelings.

CHAPTER 8

Try to see it my way

———

'No one at work takes me seriously.'

'Why do we always end up shouting at each other?'

'It's never the right moment to ask her anything difficult.'

Wouldn't life be easier if you could always persuade other people to agree with you and do things the way you wanted? There would be no more squabbles with your partner or family about where to go on holiday or whose turn it was to do the washing up. What's more, you could convince your boss to pay you what you're worth, and you'd spend much less time in meetings endlessly trying to reach a decision. Unfortunately, other people being what they are, this ideal scenario is unlikely ever to become reality.

You have to face the fact that the people you're trying to convince may simply believe that they're right and you're wrong or, worse still, refuse to give way for reasons that have nothing much to do with the rights and wrongs of the situation at all. They may be worried about losing face, getting back at you for some past slight, or in a bad mood because of something unrelated to the matter in hand – whatever it is, sweet reason is unlikely to shift them.

Anyone who expects to get their own way all the time is in for a lot of disappointment, but you should expect to come out the winner at least some of the time. And if you're someone who ends up losing out more often than not, you need to try and develop some new approaches that will increase your chances of success.

ARE YOU GETTING THROUGH?

When you want to bring others round to your point of view, you have to look at the task from two different angles. As well as marshalling all the ammunition at your disposal, you have to consider what the obstacles are. This means trying to understand in advance why the other person may resist your proposals and assessing how your message is being received as the discussion progresses. In both cases, of course, what you say and how you put it will be very important, but as we've already seen, words are only part of the message transmitted and picked up during any kind of conversation. The most logical arguments in the world will rarely succeed by themselves, and especially not if they are contradicted by other aspects of your behaviour, and above all by your body language. So you not only have to be convincing, you have to *look* convincing too. What this means is that you must try and ensure that your words and body language are what psychologists call 'congruent' – that is they are saying the same thing. First, consider what kind of approach is most likely to be effective in a particular situation, and with the person or people involved. For example, you would take a different attitude in a one-to-one encounter with a boss whom you basically like and admire from when you are dealing with a committee of strangers who you suspect will be hostile to your ideas.

● **Do you need to demonstrate your authority or capabilities?**
  In a work situation where you are dealing with a colleague you know well, you may not need to make a point of your status and your claim to be taken seriously. Unless you can be sure of this, however, it is worth taking some trouble to establish your credentials. As we saw in chapter 5, you are in a stronger position when any meeting is held on your own

territory and the arrangements are under your control. If you expect the encounter to be difficult, don't neglect the various pointers which can subtly emphasise your authority. As well as having the other person come to you, you could arrange for them to be shown in by an assistant, be on the phone or working on an important-looking document when they arrive, seat them on the other side of your desk and so on.

- **Is your aim to show that you're a worthwhile investment?** You may be asking the bank manager for a loan, trying to increase your mortgage or wanting to convince your boss that you are entitled to a salary increase. They have the power to give or withhold something you want, so your objective must be to convince them that you are worthy of their trust. Most people don't react well to whingeing and

Confident communication.

161

wheedling so you have to appear confident and capable without being arrogant. This means sitting in a relaxed but not over-casual way, looking directly at the other person while saying your piece – without trying to stare them out, of course – and keeping your behaviour sexually neutral. Fidgeting, shifting about constantly, playing with pens or paperclips will reveal nervousness, so you should try to keep your hands relatively still. It may help to remember that you are not just a supplicant depending on the other person's goodwill: they have something to gain potentially by agreeing to your request and your task is to help them to see the benefit of doing so.

- **Do you need to stand out in a crowd?**
It is probably true that the more people there are in a meeting or on a committee, the harder it will be for you to get your point across. A good chairperson will make sure that everyone with something to contribute is drawn into the discussion, but if that doesn't happen, you will have to make the effort to intervene on your own. One study in the USA found that you are more likely to be taken notice of in a group situation if you stand out in some way. For example, being the only black person or the only woman in a group makes other people see you as more influential than if you are similar to everyone else present. The researchers concluded that even though you probably cannot control the make-up of the group to suit your convenience, you can increase your visibility, and therefore your influence, by dressing or acting differently from the rest.

- **Is friendly persuasion your best bet?**
Sometimes honey is more effective than vinegar. A person who is not susceptible to reason or unwilling to accept another point of view will often co-operate simply because they like and trust you. Some psychologists define a persuasive individual as one who is liked and trusted by others and

who gets their way by fostering an atmosphere of openness. Of course, if this kind of behaviour comes naturally to you, you'll already know how effective it can be in swinging others round to your point of view. Conversely, someone whose natural approach is more combative may have to work harder to make a success of this tactic. The problem is that most people realise if you're just putting on a friendly face, and will probably feel you're trying to con them. A genuinely likeable person will look relaxed, smile a lot, and show by their expression that they really are interested in the other person's viewpoint. Facial expressions can be faked to some degree, but if the feelings aren't sincere, your posture, hand movements and tone of voice are likely to give you away. At the very least, other people will feel uncomfortable or sense that something is not quite right, even if they can't put their finger on the reason. So unless you can adopt the right approach from the inside out, friendly persuasion could lose you more than it gains.

KEEPING YOUR COOL

Shouting and losing your temper has little to recommend it as a strategy for getting what you want. It is on a par with raising your voice when talking to a foreigner in the belief that he will be more likely to understand your language. If the person you're talking to responds by shouting and screaming as well, absolutely nothing will be resolved. If, on the other hand, they allow you to rant on while remaining calm themselves, you will almost certainly come off worse.

While the classic view is that women are more likely to resort to this sort of behaviour than men, one study came to the opposite conclusion. Couples were asked to try and persuade their partners to change their mind about something. The men apparently saw this as a test of the balance of power in the relationship, so that failure would seem like a loss of status and dominance. This turned the exercise into one where there had to be a winner and a loser, and because this put them under pressure, the men were prone to become emotional and lose their temper. What they perceived as a failure made them feel inadequate – and also caused their blood pressure to rise! The women on the other hand did not see the exercise as a challenge or as any threat to their status, and were able to remain much more calm and collected. As far as they were concerned, failure to change their partner's mind said more about his stubbornness than their powers of persuasion.

Incidentally, while controlling your own temper, don't miss any clues which suggest that the other person is on the point of losing theirs. Speaking more loudly or even shouting, clenching and unclenching the fists, thrusting out the chest and getting generally rather puffed-up, together with easily recognised facial expressions such as frowning and bared teeth, are high on the list of giveaways.

While some people do smash a path for themselves by sheer aggression, most of us would prefer not to operate in this way. No one likes being shouted at, and negativity generally is not an effective technique of persuasion. For example, various health campaigns which relied on scare tactics, such as some of those designed to discourage smoking or increase awareness of HIV have not worked. Making people feel anxious or guilty is usually counter-productive, and their response is to become defensive or hostile rather than to change their ways. In these kind of campaigns, as in any attempt to change behaviour, stressing the potential benefits and rewards is more likely to achieve results.

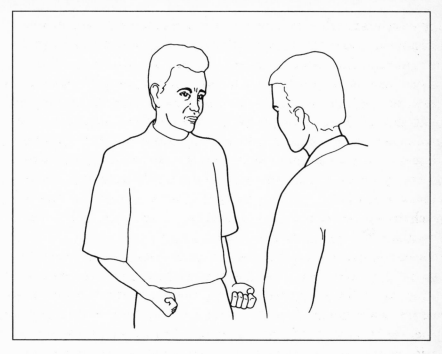

Clenched fists reveal anger.

VOICING YOUR OPINIONS

Your voice is an instrument which you already play on naturally to signify shifts in feeling, meaning and attitudes. The non-verbal components of speech – your tone of voice, its resonance, pitch and pace – are referred to by psychologists as 'paralanguage'. How you employ it can have a considerable effect on how much notice your listeners take of you.

Polish up your paralanguage
● While shouting isn't recommended, raising the volume a little is a way of emphasising and drawing attention to more important points, especially if you don't normally speak very loudly.

165

- Of course you need to speak loudly enough to be heard, but a relatively soft voice which the other person has to make a slight effort to hear clearly can be a means of ensuring that you have their complete attention. Don't let it get so soft it sounds breathy, however – most people will interpret this as a sign of nervousness or submission.

- When you want to be assertive, you need to sound confident and forceful, without turning the volume up too high. You will come over as confident if your voice is animated and expressive and your speech is fluent.

- The ideal is to talk reasonably fast, although without gabbling, because this is associated by most people with intelligence and competence. Aim to present your arguments without slowing down and with the minimum of pauses or 'ums and ahs'. For one thing, there'll be less chance that anyone will interrupt before you've finished, and for another it will make you sound more convincing.

- Avoid using too many of the polite words and phrases designed to weaken the effect of what you say. If you're telling your boss you deserve a salary increase, come out with what you mean. Say, 'I deserve more money because I've taken on new responsibilities . . .' rather than, 'I thought it might perhaps be time to talk about an increase because . . .'

LEARN THE ART OF COMPROMISE

In the real world, most attempts at persuasion end with both sides giving a little to reach a conclusion that's acceptable to both. Bashing on in the hope of winning all the points may mean you lose the game altogether. Your chances of reaching agreement will decrease if the discussion is allowed to degenerate into open confrontation or hostility. When you want to avoid provoking outright opposition, it will help if you main-

166

tain a relaxed and unaggressive posture yourself. Apart from
avoiding obvious moves such as banging the desk or wagging
your finger at the other person, you need to make sure they can
see that you're listening to their views and taking in what
they're saying. Listeners look at the other person a lot while
they're talking, and constantly give small signs – such as nods
and brief comments – to indicate that they're paying attention.
Leaning forward, with your arms relaxed and not folded to
'protect' your body will show that you're not looking for a
fight.

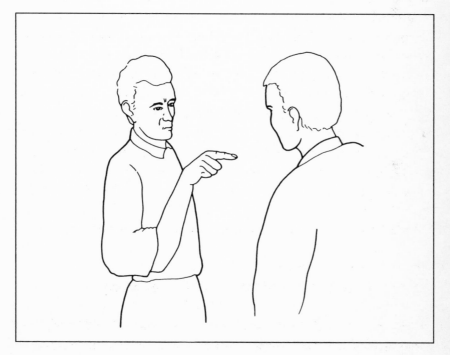

Pointing a finger at someone reveals aggression and authoritarianism.

While you're doing all you can to keep the encounter on an
even keel, you'll be watching to see what effect your behaviour
is having. In essence, you want the other person to start

167

mirroring your posture and gestures, showing that they too are in a receptive mood and not hostile or confrontational. You may need to use other tactics if you can see that, despite your efforts, he or she is still maintaining a defensive posture and showing no sign of moving towards acceptance of your point of view. Because body language not only reflects our feelings but actually influences them as well, it can help to make a movement or behave in a way which forces the other person to adopt a different position and react differently. For example, when dealing with someone who persistently leans away from you, arms folded and eyes focused anywhere but on you, you could try handing over a file or other relevant item. This will make them lean forward, unfold their arms, and eye contact will be encouraged as you explain or ask their opinion about the

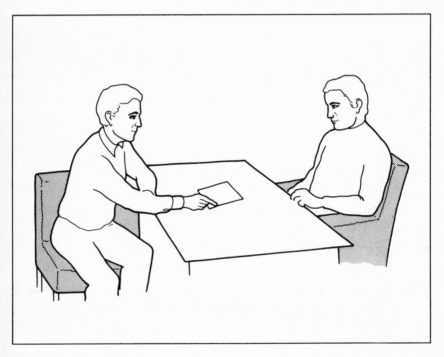

Handing over a document to focus attention.

168

material under discussion. At this point, it may help to move nearer, or perhaps come round to their side of the desk so that you are in a cooperative position rather than a competitive one.

CHOOSING YOUR MOMENT

When it's important that your boss, your partner or whoever, agrees to something you want, don't neglect the obvious. There have been numerous studies which confirm what we all know instinctively but sometimes forget: your chances of success will depend a lot on the mood the other person is in. This can be affected to a significant degree even by something as mundane as the weather.

In a study of people's behaviour called 'Weather, mood and helping . . . experiments with the Sunshine Samaritan', psychologist Michael Cunningham asked people in a city street to respond to a survey questionnaire. He found that they were more willing to cooperate in winter on a sunny day that wasn't too cold, while in summer they were more responsive on days when it wasn't too hot or humid. So don't leap on someone who has obviously got frozen or soaked on the way home from the office, when all they can think of is how to get warm and dry again. Most people are more helpful and open to new ideas in the morning, when they are fresh, rather than late in the afternoon when they're feeling tired and looking forward to going home.

Another factor which has been found to influence decisions is whether someone is feeling satisfied with themselves. The warm feeling created by winning a squash game or making a successful business deal will make the person more favourably disposed to agree to what you ask, provided you ask them fairly soon afterwards. Of course, you may not know the reason why someone is feeling good, but you should have no trouble spotting the signs if you know them at all well. Occasionally, you may be forced into a situation where you have to make a particular request, even though you can tell that it's precisely the wrong moment. When you're dealing with someone who has just suffered a defeat you need to recognise that they may feel an urge to compensate by asserting themselves and refusing to accept whatever you are proposing. You will know from the frowns, 'dominant' postures and unfriendly demeanour, that success is unlikely by normal methods, so this could be the time to resort to a more submissive approach. It's worth trying the opposites of the tactics described above – making a point of going into the other person's territory and letting them lead the encounter. This means you are the one making the effort to please, looking anxious and avoiding a confident, self-assured posture. If you couple this with an approach that stresses your need for the other's person's help or support and your dependence on their goodwill, you will be boosting their deflated ego. Agreeing to your request offers a way to restore their sense of power which a more straightforward approach could not provide. You may not enjoy having to give this performance, but there are times when it can serve your purpose. Another approach is to present your request in the form of an appeal to the other's person's authority or ingenuity: 'I wonder if you are able to help me . . .?' or, 'Do you think you have enough influence with the Chairman to . . .?' If skilfully worded, your question may motivate the other person to help so they can demonstrate their potency.

CHAPTER 9

Beat the cheats

———

'I never know when he's telling the truth.'
'Why am I such a hopeless liar?'
'You can't trust her – she's got a shifty look.'

Lying gets a bad press. No one likes to be accused of it, much less caught doing it, and we all hate discovering that someone has deliberately deceived us. Even in the House of Commons, where MPs indulge in all manner of insults, calling another Member a liar is beyond the pale. Naturally, they can usually find more subtle ways of implying that a colleague has been 'economical with the actualité' as a Cabinet Secretary once elegantly put it. Yet despite the high value we put on truthfulness, all of us tell lies some of the time. Can you put your hand on your heart and say that an untruth has not passed your lips in the last twenty-four hours? What about the last week?

Everyday lies range from the familiar 'the cheque's in the post' to the tactful 'I like your new hairstyle', and from covering up an affair to concealing details of your lovelife from your parents. Most people make a distinction between white lies, told to avoid hurting someone's feelings, and serious deception. And they are almost certainly right to do so. Imagine what life would be like if everyone was compelled to be totally honest all the time. Social and family life, not to mention the smooth running of the workplace, would be totally disrupted as everyone had to face the reality of what others thought of their clothes, cooking, girlfriend, telephone manner and lunch invitation, without the protection of those little white lies. Sometimes we even connive at being lied to, because it's easier to accept a half-convincing excuse than face the fact that a friend really doesn't want to come to stay because she can't stand your partner, or that you're being moved to another job because you get on your boss's nerves.

WHY PEOPLE TELL LIES

There's more to lying than just saving people's feelings, and we do it for a variety of reasons. For most of us it's a way of dealing with a crisis situation – whether major or very minor – and is employed only rarely, but for others it can become as natural as breathing. Why do we lie? Here are some of our motivations.

1 **Self-protection**
   A few people will confess when caught doing something they shouldn't be doing, but many more will lie and protest their innocence. This ranges from situations such as actual crimes to more mundane misdemeanours such as spilling coffee on a carpet or making a personal phone call from work. The point is usually to avoid the prospect of retribution or, at the very least, losing face or popularity.
2 **Part of the job**
   Some occupations make it either necessary or expedient to lie at times. At one extreme is the undercover agent – policeman or customs' officer or member of the security services, for example – and at the other the assistant in a clothes shop who persuades a customer that the garment they've just tried on looks perfect. You might also include in this category the confidence tricksters who will often act the part so well that they actually believe in it themselves.
3 **Loyalty**
   Some people would lie rather than admit they, or someone they're close to, have done something disreputable or have

174

faults which they don't want to admit. For example, someone accused of passing on a secret they promised to keep may deny having said a word to a single soul, because they know they shouldn't have.

4 **Buying time**

This can happen when someone feels under pressure to make a decision or a commitment before they've had a chance to really think through what response they want to make. It may be something quite minor, like a social arrangement, or it might be a situation where a great deal hangs on the answer. For example, a prospective employer may tell an anxious applicant that the decision hasn't yet been made about a job offer, when actually they're waiting to see whether their first choice says yes or no.

HOW CAN YOU TELL?

You may believe that you're one of those people who knows instinctively when you're being lied to, but the chances are you're wrong. In a recent TV interview Aldrich Ames, the American CIA officer convicted of selling secrets to the USSR over many years during the Cold War, told an interesting story. When there were rumours flying of a possible traitor inside the organisation (but before Ames came under suspicion) he was discussing the effectiveness of lie detectors (or polygraphs) with a female colleague. She declared she had no use for them as she could always spot a liar. 'I have a kind of sixth sense,' she blandly assured him, oblivious that the man she was talking to had been lying through his teeth for the past decade. She perhaps didn't entirely deserve his amused contempt, however, as he seemed in the interview to be completely unembarrassed about his life of deception or its consequences. He had sold secrets for money, not from political conviction, and showed no overt sign of the guilt or remorse which might have led him to betray himself.

Identifying a traitor is only one example of a situation where the ability to recognise dishonesty would be invaluable. The police, criminal juries, politicians and even spouses suspicious of their partner's faithfulness would give a great deal for an infallible means of lie detection, and most of us would find it helpful in everyday life. But no such reliable system has yet been invented or discovered, so we have to rely on picking up what clues we can. Much research has been devoted to studying the non-verbal ways in which we reveal our duplicity, as well as what makes some people better liars than others. In experiments, people were asked to answer questions untruthfully, to lie to 'patients' about the severity of their illnesses, to describe people they liked as if they didn't like them, or to smuggle drugs past 'customs inspectors'. To make sure that the 'subjects' had a motive to do well in the tasks they were set, they were often told that it was a test of skill or that they would be paid for results. In one study, the participants were also given other psychological questionnaires to see whether these supplied any clues as to what kind of personality makes a successful liar.

Practising to deceive

Research by the Californian psychologist Paul Ekman and his colleagues have pinpointed certain visible changes in the body language of people who have been asked to lie. The findings were not necessarily what you might have expected, in that our faces are not as good at revealing the truth as other elements over which we have less control.

- **Gestures** – in normal conversation, you use your hands to emphasise and clarify the meaning or significance of what you're saying, even if you're not quite in the same league as the natives of Naples who are said to become dumb if their hands are tied. Nevertheless, even though you may not be aware of how you normally use your hands, you will probably use them less when you're not telling the truth. It's almost as though your hands are refusing to have any part in your deception. Some people will literally sit on their hands in this situation, while others grasp them firmly together or stuff them deep inside their pockets. This seems to come out of a recognition that hand gestures are very closely related to thought and speech and hence might give away more than you intended. As we saw earlier, keeping your arms relaxed and showing your palms are ways of showing openness and goodwill, which don't feel right while you're telling lies.

Hiding hands and the truth.

● **Touching** – while most people use fewer gestures when lying, it is almost impossible to keep your hands completely still, and instead of waving them around you probably touch your face more often than usual. The classic indicator of a lie is sometimes said to be the hand hovering over or near the mouth. This is a diluted version of the way a child will clasp both hands over his or her mouth after telling a whopper – as adults we learn not to be quite so obvious but don't eliminate the movement entirely. Variations on this theme include rubbing your nose, stroking your chin and pulling at your earlobe – all attempts to cover up a lie which is causing you some kind of inner conflict. Psychologists believe that it is probably tension which brings your hands into action, and makes them adopt a protective position. You may cover your eyes or nose (in a similar way to a boxer putting up his guard) as though anticipating a physical attack. After all, the face and especially the eyes are among the most important and vulnerable parts of your body.

Give-away gestures.

178

- **Hand shrugging** – this is another way your hands escape from your conscious control and try to tell your listener that things are not what they seem. Again, it is as though your hands were disclaiming responsibility for what your voice is doing.

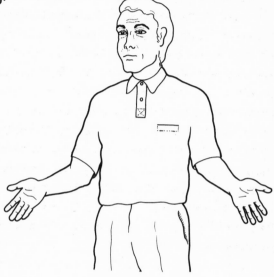

Hand shrugging.

- **Fidgeting** – the further down your body you go, the less successful your attempts at control are likely to be, so you may well keep crossing or uncrossing your legs or shifting your position. Sometimes you'll notice your feet pointing towards the nearest exit – as if anxious to carry you away from the scene of the deception. However, squirming and fidgeting by themselves are not enough to give you away because these movements are also seen in someone who is simply tense or uneasy but not necessarily lying.
- **Facial expressions** – the need to wear a mask to cover your true feelings in some situations means you've probably developed a certain amount of skill at controlling your face. Nevertheless, some clues to your real thoughts and feelings

179

may flicker across your features before you know it's happened. Slow-motion photography can reveal these fleeting micro-expressions which sometimes last only a fraction of a second and vanish before you know it. Psychologists explain this phenomenon in terms of division of labour within your brain – one part sets off the natural expression initially, then a higher brain centre quickly moves in to cancel it, effectively telling the face to shut up! The change is so swift that other people are unlikely to register it consciously, but they may still have the sense that something's wrong even though they don't know what. In fact, these micro-expressions do occur when you're lying, but they can also appear when you're uncertain or undecided about what you're saying – perhaps because you haven't yet made up your mind how you think or feel about the subject under discussion or the person you're talking to.

- **Eye contact** – most people find it hard to look someone in the eye while deliberately lying to them. This is why we tend to mistrust 'shifty-eyed individuals'. As well as looking away from the other person more than usual, a liar will often turn away completely and will also blink more frequently. Beware of placing too much stress on this kind of signal by itself, however. As with other kinds of 'lying behaviour', they are actually manifestations of discomfort or unease which may have other, more innocent, explanations.

- **Sounding sincere** – the stress of telling a porkie is likely to come through in your voice, irrespective of the words you're using. For one thing, you'll hesitate more and your voice may lose much of its expressiveness, so that it sounds rather flat and monotonous. Some people can't help speaking in a more high-pitched tone when telling untruths. An interesting experiment was tried a couple of years ago as part of the annual National Science Week. The idea was to test whether people could recognise deception more readily when it was

180

perpetrated on TV, in a newspaper or on the radio. Surprisingly, more people recognised that they were being lied to when they simply heard the speaker's voice on the radio.

Voice prints (the frequency analysis of speech sounds) also betray anxiety and stress, and under certain conditions, these may be interpreted as signs of guilt or an attempt to deceive. On an amateur level, many women with unreliable partners can tell from a phone call whether he really is 'working late at the office' as he claims or just covering up something more disreputable.

MOTIVATION MATTERS

As we've said, spotting a liar is much harder than most people think, and the picture is complicated still further by the results of some specialised research projects. These looked at people who were described as very highly motivated to lie – such as confidence tricksters or high-pressure salespeople might be in real life. When it comes to eye contact, for instance, such people know very well that looking shifty will render them suspect, so they try hard to override the natural tendency to look away. Instead of glancing off somewhere else, they tend to exaggerate the normal amount of eye contact and will stare you straight in the face while delivering their lie. At the same time, they will be taking pains to avoid blinking and squirming, because they know that these too are tell-tale signs. Making better known the results of research into the way liars' body language gives them away can simply compound the difficulty of recognising the signals if this results in tricksters adapting their behaviour. Those on the receiving end of their lies need to take account of this and look for magnified 'honesty signals' instead.

181

In the light of these findings, it is interesting to look at what cues most people use when they are trying to detect lying. In order of importance, the main ones are:

1 Slowness to begin talking
2 Looking away
3 More postural shifts
4 Pausing while talking
5 Smiling less
6 Speaking more slowly
7 Using a higher-pitched tone of voice
8 Making mistakes in speech

Some of these really are reliable – such as raised pitch and speaking more slowly – but the others can be deliberately overridden by a would-be deceiver. Some which are worth watching for in this kind of person are:

- dilated pupils
- blinking less than normal
- fewer head movements
- speaking in relatively short bursts

What is revealed by this research is a complex game of second-guessing in which the liar tries to suppress the giveaway signs of deceit and the judge looks either for direct signs of lying or for blatant attempts to disguise the appearance of lying. As people learn more about body language, the more sophisticated they become at covering up their lying. Whereas a child simply hides his mouth behind his hand and can be easily seen through as a result by most adults, with adults themselves we have to look for more subtle signs of 'leakage'.

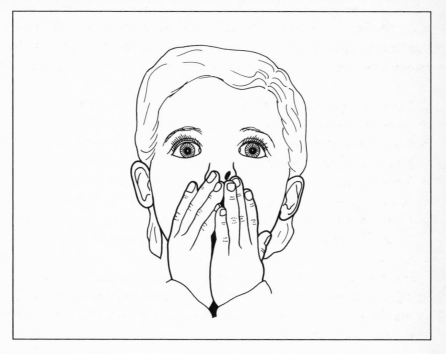

A child lying.

The lie detector
The lie detector (or polygraph) is used very little in this country but is more acceptable in the USA where it is used on people accused of crimes or those being screened for security reasons. Of course, it doesn't measure 'lying' as such; rather it works on physical changes which are said to accompany lying. The idea is that the emotional stress of lying will produce physical effects which the individual can't control and it is these changes which the polygraph measures. Through special sensors attached to the subject's body, the machine records changes in heart-rate, breathing and sweat-gland activity. While this continuous measurement is going on, the subject is asked three different types of question:

183

- unemotional
- emotional, but irrelevant to the crime or the matter at issue
- relevant to the crime or issue

The most important comparison is between the responses to the second and third categories of question, and is more likely to be valid when innocent respondents have no way of knowing which questions are relevant and which not. The problem is that people's reactions are not always consistent or uniform. Innocent individuals may show signs of stress simply because the circumstances make them nervous; but it is not unknown for 'guilty' parties, like the CIA traitor Aldrich Ames mentioned above, to pass a polygraph test with flying colours.

Some psychopaths are virtually devoid of any guilt feelings, hence newer techniques are being developed which only consider the question of whether the suspect's brain recognises certain crime-related words or articles.

GOOD AND BAD LIARS

Does your personality have any effect on whether you can lie convincingly? According to a study carried out by psychologists in California, the answer is yes. The project gave a series of personality tests to a group of people who were then asked to give a series of short talks to two panels of judges. The talks were chosen so that each speaker gave one where they genuinely believed in what they were saying, one where they profoundly disagreed and a third about which they were neutral. The judges were then asked to rate them for 'believability'. The people they seemed most inclined to believe in all three situations were the ones whose personality tests showed them to be particularly outgoing, warm, impulsive, happy-go-lucky, enthusiastic, bold and energetic. Their performance was seen

184

by the panels as simply more believable. The researchers also found that those people who were anxious to come across favourably to others seemed to be able to present themselves in a socially acceptable way and were thus more likely to be believed. Another group who scored well on believability when they were actually not being honest were those whose personality tests showed them to be very self-controlled and self-disciplined. The researchers suggested that this might be because they were better able to mask their anxiety and so gave fewer clues through their body language. Prominent among the 'bad liars' were people whose personality tests showed they were prone to feeling anxious, guilty or apprehensive and so more likely to give themselves away.

'I CANNOT TELL A LIE'

Even though you are generally an honest person and dislike telling lies, there are times when the truth may not be appropriate. When you feel that the situation makes a lie unavoidable, you have to do your best to be convincing or there's no point in lying at all.

- Take a tip from the professionals. Actors usually work from the inside out – in other words, they conjure up the appropriate emotion from something in their own experience which they then express through their body language. In everyday life, you will be a more convincing liar if you can first convince yourself. Because many of the clues people recognise as signs of lying are actually really demonstrating an inner conflict which the person is trying to conceal, eliminating this conflict is the ideal way to appear believable. For this reason, the best advice to liars is that they should always make their fictional story as close to the

185

truth as possible, only changing certain critical details.

- Remember that most amateur liars have more control over their facial expressions than over other aspects of their body language. So if you know you're going to have to lie, it may help to position yourself in such a way that some of your body at least is concealed from your listener – say behind a large desk, for example.

  Alternatively, you could try to arrange to be involved in some other task at the same time – perhaps preparing a meal or using the photocopier!

- Most people find it difficult to believe that someone who has a pleasant expression and smiles a lot could be lying. So try to manage plenty of smiles, provided you can do it with a fair amount of naturalness. At the same time, bear in mind that you shouldn't smile when it is inappropriate – for example, when appealing on TV for the safe return of a spouse you have pushed off a cliff!

- Make a point of looking at the person you're lying to instead of following your instinct and turning away, which will immediately make them feel uneasy.

- Don't lie unless you really have to. As we've seen, the more highly motivated you are, the more likely you are to carry through your deception convincingly.

NOBODY DOES IT BETTER . . .

Expert liars are very highly motivated to be convincing. What makes it more difficult for them is that their audiences often start with a high index of suspicion – we automatically distrust someone who is trying to sell us something, whether it's a political party line or a secondhand car. Those who are most successful frequently use a combination of psychology and acting techniques. They make conscious use of 'honest' body language, being well aware of the clues which would give away their deception and deliberately suppressing them. It also helps if they begin by convincing themselves, at least temporarily. A salesman who has genuinely persuaded himself that he is offering the bargain of all time will be more effective than one who knows he's selling a pig in a poke. You'd be lucky if you were able to pick up any clues from someone like this at all.

In any case, you have to be wary of making a judgement on the basis of too little evidence. You'd be right to doubt someone who manifested most or all of the signs we've described, but one or two clues by themselves could easily be misinterpreted. Hand movements or micro-expressions, for instance, might indicate a lie, but they could also mean that the person is worried or stressed because they're unsure of what to say. You have a better chance of detecting deception with someone very close to you, because any deviation from their normal behaviour is more immediately recognisable. And, of course, the same thing applies in reverse. Your nearest and dearest are more likely to catch you out in a lie than someone who knows you less well.

CHAPTER 10

Who's under stress?

———

'I do badly in interviews because I get so nervous.'

'She never sits still when she's talking to you.'

'He was so embarrassed and I just made things worse.'

One thing at least is certain about stress – there's a lot of it about these days. Many of us feel under all kinds of pressure because of the lives we lead, and that doesn't just apply to the high-flying executive or 'top person' who was once seen as the most likely victim. Having too much to do in too little time can certainly create stress, but it's likely to be less severe than the kind which results from having no job, too little money and no way of changing the situation.

Most of us tend to perceive stress in a negative way – blaming it for everything from forgetfulness to irritability, from colds to cancer. So before we start to look at how you can spot the signs in yourself and others, we should first try and define what we mean by stress.

What is stress?

Despite our fundamentally negative view of it, stress can be a positive element in certain circumstances. Without it, some people would never get out of bed nor be able to achieve all the things they want or need to do. The physical and mental consequences can drive you into acting or responding to a given situation, and though you may not enjoy the feeling particularly, at least it has served a purpose.

How you respond to stress depends partly on your personality – what's intolerable to one person is stimulating to another. But there can come a point in anyone's life where the stress is simply overwhelming and prevents you from functioning effectively. In general, people can cope with higher levels of stress when they feel that they are in control of their own lives – of their behaviour and decisions – and can influence what happens to them. When it all becomes too much you may well feel trapped by circumstances, with few or perhaps no choices. The result is you feel overwhelmed and unable to cope, and unless the situation improves, you can all too easily end up in a downward spiral.

The first signs
- You get irritable with other people
- You grumble and moan a lot
- You're prone to flare up and lose your temper over nothing
- You put things off
- You worry about the future

You may also notice some physical symptoms, such as unexplained twitching, having to go to the loo more often and chest pains. If the stress isn't relieved, these early problems can develop into continual minor ailments, such as colds, indigestion, headaches, eczema and other skin problems.

Perhaps the most wearing symptom of stress is constant anxiety, even when you're not worrying about anything specific. This is because your body is responding to stress by releasing more of the so-called 'flight-or-fight' hormone adrenaline into your bloodstream to prepare you for action which doesn't come. This adrenaline surge came in very handy in the days when humans were constantly faced with new and unexpected physical dangers, but today we aren't often called on to flee or do battle with sabre-toothed tigers. This feeling of

192

being constantly in a state of alarm from which there is no relief through violent physical activity can leave you feeling on edge and unable to relax. If it goes on for too long, you develop other symptoms in response, such as insomnia, tearfulness, loss of concentration and energy and a permanent sense of being unable to cope.

As well as feeling physically under par and constantly on their guard against they know not what, the person who is not coping with stress will start to behave differently towards other people. For one thing, they may talk either more or less than usual, but their conversation is likely to focus almost exclusively on their worries. They naturally see only the down side and seem to be making no effort to deal with the problems they're facing. Often they make it hard for other people to help because they become withdrawn and inclined to snap at anyone who tries to offer advice or support.

Of course, these are extreme reactions to prolonged and unrelieved stress, and fortunately the majority of people don't ever get to that stage. However, if you see yourself – or someone close to you – beginning to head down that track, you must find some way of interrupting the downward slide. Many GPs are well-informed and sympathetic to people suffering from stress, and your local surgery or health centre is probably the best place to start seeking help. The doctor may recommend relaxation techniques or classes, approaches such as yoga or, if the problem is really severe, some form of counselling.

NO WAY TO HIDE

As we've seen, the 'flight-or-fight' response to stress is a physical one, and is under the control of the sympathetic nervous system. The changes it induces to prepare you for action aren't under your conscious control, and so the bodily

193

signs are difficult if not impossible to conceal from a careful observer. Since you can't alter them, just accept that they will occur and do what you can to counter their effects. If you're facing a task which makes you nervous, such as giving a speech, you're bound to experience a reaction. Even actors or others who are used to performing in public feel on edge beforehand. Indeed many would say that this adrenaline response helps them to perform their task better because without it their reactions would be slower and they would create less of an impact. So try not to let your physical response worry you in a situation like this, because it is perfectly normal and generally others will sympathise rather than criticise you for it.

Stress signals
- The surge of adrenaline affects your circulation, causing your heart to beat faster.
- The blood drains from the surface of your body to the muscles and brain, ensuring that they have all the oxygen they may need to deal with the perceived crisis. As a result, your face may be noticeably paler than usual. Many TV performers counteract this effect with make-up, and obviously a woman can do the same thing if she knows she's going to face a stressful situation. More often than not, however, the stress arises unexpectedly so there's no chance to apply this kind of disguise. Remember, though, that the effect is only temporary and your skin tone will return to normal once your body accepts that the need for physical preparedness is past.
- You start to breathe faster and more deeply to increase your oxygen intake. The movement of your chest will be visible to anyone who cares to look for it, and you may feel you don't have sufficient breath to speak normally. It helps if you can make a conscious effort to breathe more smoothly – take a few slow, deep breaths before you start to talk.

- Your sweat glands leap into action to cool you down so you perspire more. This feels uncomfortable, but it may not be as obvious as you fear, unless you really are sweating buckets.
- Your digestive system shuts down for the duration and the supply of saliva is reduced, so your mouth feels dry. Sipping from a glass of water will help, if this is possible, and using some kind of lip balm may stop you from licking your lips in an attempt to moisten them.

Fortunately, perhaps, our bodies do not remain in this state of heightened arousal indefinitely. Once the immediate threat is past – or if nothing happens – other parts of the autonomic nervous system take over and attempt to settle everything down again. You may then feel rather peculiar for a while as the various bodily changes reverse themselves. Your face may flush as the blood returns, for example, the saliva comes back into your mouth, and you may need to rush to the loo. This is the time when you're most liable to feel faint, rather than in the heat of the crisis as you might expect. Knowing the order in which these changes occur, and what they mean, can be useful when you're on the receiving end of someone else's stress. An individual who's puffed up with anger and red in the face is certainly alarming, but they probably offer less of a real threat than if they were tense and deadly pale. As we've seen, pallor is one indication that the person is geared up to fight if necessary, so they are more likely to lash out – physically or verbally – than the one who's purple with fury.

WHAT'S REALLY GOING ON

Finding the right way to deal with someone who's under stress isn't easy because they are usually not in any state to respond. For example, when you need to resolve a problem at work with a colleague who is being obstructive or unresponsive, you'll have a better chance of success if you can work out what's bugging him or her. Similarly, if a friend or relative is uncommunicative or awkward, you need to know whether the problem has to do with something you've said or done, or whether their behaviour is prompted by someone or something else entirely. Many of the signs you're picking up could be explained in several ways, so you need to look at the whole picture and try to sort out what's wrong. For instance, someone who continually puts a hand up to their face, touching their nose or covering their mouth may be feeling stressed because they are not sure what to say, or for some other reason, or they may be embarrassed because they feel they're making a fool of themselves. If you can sense when someone is anxious, you can

Stress and anxiety.

take steps to reassure them, whereas otherwise you might just feel that they disliked you or would rather be somewhere else. To some extent, of course, feelings may overlap. If you are a patient trying to explain to your doctor that you have intimate symptoms which you fear are caused by some sinister disease, you may feel embarrassed and anxious at the same time. As the doctor, you may be under stress because the waiting room is full of patients and also because you have to give someone bad news about their health. Nevertheless, there are some subtle differences in body language which can help you to sort out what the other person is feeling.

1 **All stressed out**: As we saw earlier, people who are labouring under a large load of stress often feel overwhelmed and desperate to escape any more pressure. It's not surprising, therefore, that their body language will often reflect this need directly.

- frequent or prolonged blinking which actually has the effect of blocking visual input. Like a child who covers his eyes and thinks you can't see him, an overstressed person will often close their eyes for seconds at a time or actually cover them with their hands.
- avoiding eye contact or letting their eyes flicker constantly away from the person they're talking to may reflect a general wish to escape any more social interaction. However, unless you are aware that this is the case, you're likely to take it personally and assume it's you they want to get away from. As we saw in chapter 1, avoiding eye contact is often a way of demonstrating a lack of interest in the other person and it can also be a clue to lying. It's important to remember that it needs to be interpreted in the light of other clues if you are to avoid misunderstandings.

197

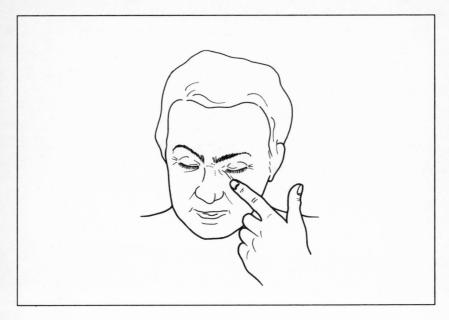

Blocking visual input by rubbing an eye.

- touching or pulling on an ear or even covering the ears with both hands as if to shut out difficult questions or avoid the necessity of talking. This can be an unconscious way of saying, 'I've heard enough.'
- touching or scratching the nose is something many people do when faced with a difficult question. However, when under stress, the nerve endings in the nose may tingle and rubbing or scratching is the natural response.
- fidgeting, fiddling with buttons, tapping fingers or feet, are all indications that someone is agitated. Bear in mind that you may not be the cause of the problem. It could just be that the person finds the general situation stressful – some people regard parties or large gatherings of any kind as something of a torment, however much they would like to be able to relax and enjoy the conversation and new encounters.

198

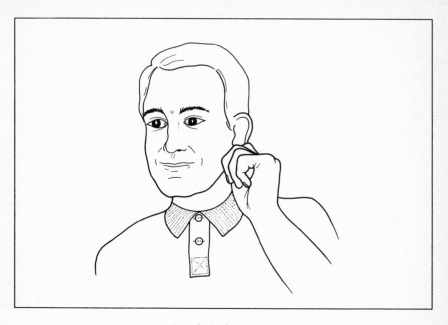

'I've heard enough!'

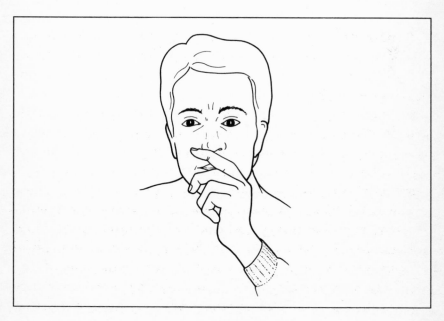

Nose scratching.

199

- adjusting cuffs or watch or finding some other acceptable way of bringing the arms across the body can be seen as a technique of 'self-defence'. It creates a barrier against the rest of the world, which is reassuring to someone who's feeling oppressed by too much of other people.

Adjusting cuffs may be a form of emotional self-defense.

2 **High anxiety**: If you are a naturally confident and outgoing person, you may find it hard to recognise when someone you meet – or even someone you know quite well – is showing signs of anxiety. It's particularly difficult when the situation doesn't seem to warrant it – chatting with a group of friendly acquaintances, for example, or discussing a job which has actually gone quite well. Unless you are alert to the real explanation, a highly anxious person can come across to you as cold or uninterested, when that's the very opposite of how

they'd like to be perceived. There have been various studies investigating the kinds of behaviour which signal anxiety and a recent one at the University of California analysed facial expression in great detail. Anxiety is a difficult emotion to recognise because it is made up of other feelings in different proportions. The anxious individual may be experiencing a cocktail of sensations, ranging from fear through apprehension and nervousness, to guilt and distress.

- Making mistakes when speaking is something most of us tend to do when we're anxious. You'll often notice it when you hear inexperienced people being interviewed on radio or TV, for example. They'll use odd grammatical structures, get quite ordinary words wrong or suddenly lose the thread of what they'd started to say. They are so worried about saying the wrong thing or, even worse, drying up completely, that their tongue seems to run away with them and they make the kind of mistakes they would never make in ordinary conversation. In this situation, the only real solution is practice: the more interviews you do, the more fluent you become. To some extent, the same is true in everyday life. If you can get used to coping in situations that make you anxious, and realise that you can get through them even if you do make the odd error, your anxiety levels will gradually decline.

- Yet again, decreased eye contact is something to watch out for. Actually looking the other person in the eye is one of the most difficult things for an anxious person to do, because they are aware that so much real communication takes place in this way. They may be afraid both of what they will read in the other person's eyes, and what their own may give away. Rather than looking round the room, they are likely to look down, but of course this is still likely to be interpreted as lack of interest unless the listener is a sensitive person and understands the real reason.

201

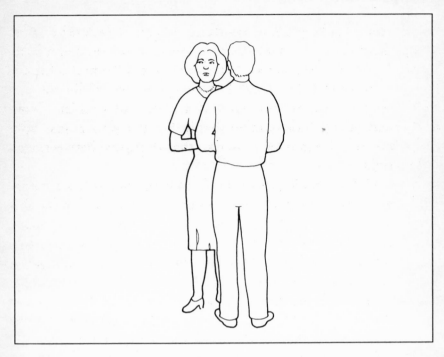

Continual avoidance of eye contact conveys lack of interest.

- Blinking more than normal is something we do when we're anxious although we're probably not aware of it. It may be that this is another attempt to minimise eye contact or to shut out information that we don't want to receive. The Californian study mentioned above found that the blink rate could double in periods of high anxiety, but pointed out that this sign needs to be taken together with other signs of anxiety because there could be other explanations for the increase. It can be rather disconcerting once you notice someone doing it, but remember that it's not something they can control, and helping them to relax is the best way of dealing with it.
- When we looked at the question of personal space in chapter 4, we pointed out that there are wide variations in what feels a comfortable distance to be from the person

you're talking to, depending on your relationship with them and, to some extent, on the culture you come from. Nevertheless, an anxious person will tend to prefer to keep a greater distance than someone who's confident and relaxed. Unless you are aware of the problem, your natural reaction will probably be to try to adjust your position by moving closer so that the space between feels right.

Unfortunately, this is likely to make things worse as the anxious person will feel threatened and respond by moving away. If the cycle isn't broken, you may end up doing a circuit round the room as one pursues and the other retreats continually. If you suspect that this is starting to happen, stop and consider why. Think about the other signs you're picking up and if it seems probable that you're dealing with an anxious person, rather than one who just wants to escape or one whose ideas of personal space are different from yours, keep still and do what you can to reassure them that you are friendly and unthreatening.

- Trying to have a conversation with someone who is constantly shifting about or squirming in their seat can quickly make you feel ill at ease as well. However, allowing your discomfort to show will only make the anxious person more tense, so try and concentrate on keeping a relaxed and open posture yourself in the hope that they will eventually calm down.
- The Californian researchers who studied facial movements in anxious people found that the greater the anxiety, the more facial movements the individuals made. In particular, they were inclined to show signs of fear, raising their eyebrows and drawing them together and stretching their mouths into an oblong shape. Once you are aware of them, these expressions are fairly easy to spot, and you can take them as your cue to offer support and reassurance or, if

necessary, steer clear of the topic which seems to be provoking an anxious response.

- It seems paradoxical, but when we are anxious, we are more rather than less inclined to smile. What we are doing the researchers claim, is giving 'non-enjoyment' smiles, as distinct from the natural expressions of happiness or amusement. A non-enjoyment smile doesn't involve the eyes, appears unexpectedly or at the wrong moment, and lasts for more or less time than a normal 'enjoyment' smile. We are trying to conceal what we're really feeling and the smile is put on like a mask to hide our anxiety, and is just about as convincing. Interestingly, the Californian study found a difference between men and women in terms of the amount of smiling each did. While both sexes showed 'non-enjoyment' smiles when feeling anxious, the women smiled less than the men as their anxiety levels increased.

- Self-comforting gestures are also more common in people who are feeling anxious. These include touching and stroking oneself, folding the arms into a cuddling position and, most obviously of all, sucking the thumb (a return to the sensation of being breast-fed?) or nail-biting (which could be a modified form of the same thing).

- Anxious people often respond in similar ways to someone who's afraid – for example, becoming frozen like a statue, opening their eyes wide as if in terror, or moving towards solid objects such as walls, fences, trees or desks for protection from imaginary predators. They may also clutch on to objects for security, treating them as teddy bear equivalents.

3 **Don't embarrass me**: Can you remember the most embarrassing thing that's ever happened to you? Each of us can probably picture at least one incident which is seared into our memory, when we just wanted the ground to open up

and swallow us. When you're a teenager, it seems to happen all the time, but as you become more confident and gain more social skills, the experience is hopefully repeated less frequently. But just what is it that makes us feel so awful? Often the incident by itself is something relatively trivial – we say the 'wrong' thing, find ourselves the centre of unwanted attention, or are clumsy with someone else's china. Whatever it is, it's not dangerous or life-threatening, or even likely to turn us into social outcasts for the rest of our lives.

Folding arms as a self-comforting gesture.

- Loss of face: this tends to happen in situations where we're keen to make a good impression, then do or say something which reveals a chasm between how we want to appear and our less acceptable selves. For instance, you might spill

205

the boss's coffee by becoming over-enthusiastic at an important meeting, faint in the middle of a crowded restaurant, or expose your ignorance in a conversation where you were trying to appear sophisticated and knowledgeable. Instead of appearing calm and in control, you suddenly feel foolish and inept, and the more flustered you become, the worse it all gets.

- Everyone's looking at you: you may be dancing away at a party when you realise everyone else has left the floor, or perhaps you're suddenly asked for your opinion in a group whose goodwill is important. Even worse (for the non-exhibitionist anyway), you're put under pressure to take your turn with the karaoke machine and can't think how to get out of it gracefully.

- Feeling a fool: you've been holding forth with great vitriol about a certain person's worst faults when it slowly dawns on you you're talking to their best friend, or you're confidently airing your in-depth knowledge about a country you've visited once only to discover you're addressing someone who's lived there for years. What all these situations (and other similar ones that are bound to spring to mind) have in common is that they bring on feelings of anxiety about the impression you're making on other people. You fear that by exposing yourself to other people by your inappropriate or clumsy behaviour, you've led them to think badly of you.

WHEN YOUR FOOT'S IN YOUR MOUTH . . .

A social gaffe may have been responsible for President Ford losing an election to Jimmy Carter in the 1970s. Ford was well ahead in a crucial TV debate when he made an inexplicably foolish statement, declaring that 'the Soviet Union does not dominate Eastern Europe'. From that point on, the body language stress indicators showed an unmistakable swing against Ford and in favour of Carter – a setback from which the President never recovered. His poll ratings plummeted from then on and he subsequently lost the election. It was not so much what Ford said that mattered as the reversal in confidence which followed and the way this was registered by the viewers.

When we've done something embarrassing, most of us make it worse for ourselves by our subsequent reactions. We blush scarlet and either mumble our apologies or try to explain, rather than just letting it go. We become agitated and look down at the floor, in a variation of the I-can't-see-you-so-you-can't-see-me ploy we've come across before. The old adage, 'Never apologise, never explain', is somewhat crude, and there are times when it is appropriate to do so, especially if you've hurt someone's feelings. Nevertheless, if the incident was really trivial you'll only draw more attention to yourself by keeping on about it. The actor Sir John Gielgud is said to be the master of this kind of situation. Famous for his social gaffes, he claims to regret them yet carries them off with considerable aplomb. Some even suspect that his *faux pas* are less accidental than they seem, but no one seems to love him any less as a result. Rather the opposite – his tendency to put his foot in his mouth is just regarded as part of his unique charm. Sadly, the rest of us are unlikely to get away with anything quite so blatant and so must make more of an effort to avoid treading on other people's toes.

It's one thing learning to handle your own feelings of embarrassment, but what can you do to help someone else who's covered in confusion? The usual reaction, at least from people who aren't revelling in someone else's discomfort, is to use what psychologists call 'dissociation exercises'. These are simply ways of covering up the incident or pretending it never happened. At first, to show that it's nothing serious, you may well laugh, then start insisting that there's absolutely no need for apologies. 'Don't worry – I'm always breaking glasses myself', or, 'My fault – I shouldn't have sprung the question on you like that', and so on. Remembering that embarrassment is actually the result of the person worrying they've made themselves socially unacceptable, your object should be to reassure them there's no need to be concerned. Smiling, looking at them a lot, or perhaps putting a hand on their arm if appropriate, will all help to reassure someone that you haven't stopped liking them.

In an ideal world, the best way to deal with stress is to solve whatever is causing it, but, of course, this isn't always possible in practice. If you, or someone close to you, seem in danger of sinking under the pressure, then do seek help before things get any worse. However, if you're one of the majority for whom stress is unavoidable sometimes but ultimately survivable, your best hope is disguise. Acting cool and calm, even – or especially – when you're not, may make some situations easier to deal with. For example, if you're facing a difficult encounter at work, perhaps with your boss or a colleague who has to be disciplined, tempers are less likely to fray if one of you at least appears to be in control of yourself. The same principles apply in family or social life. People who know you well are more likely to spot signs of tension, and may not be above exploiting it to get their own way.

SIX WAYS TO TAKE CONTROL

1 Take a few deep breaths and try to ignore the fact that your heart is beating faster than normal.
2 Make an effort to let the tension go out of your muscles – some people find it helps to deliberately clench each one in turn then let go. If you can do that, your posture will look more relaxed and less rigid.

3 However difficult you find it, try to keep looking at the person you're dealing with. Remember that looking away or down is guaranteed to make the other person react against you in some way, even if they're not sure why.

4 Don't try to appease your conversational companion by smiling unless you are sure you can do so naturally. A false smile is unmistakable and worse than none at all.

5 If you can't relax, at least try to keep reasonably still. Keep your hands away from your face and don't fiddle with your belongings, your hair or anything else.

6 When your raised levels of adrenaline are making you feel restless, and when the situation allows, it's sometimes a useful ploy to engage in some kind of physical activity such as vacuuming or cleaning the car. This burns off the adrenaline in a productive and less obvious way than simply pacing around.

CHAPTER 11

In the real world . . .

'*I must find a way to make the right impression.*'
'*He seems unfriendly, but in reality he's just shy.*'
'*I can't work out just why I didn't like her.*'

Understanding the subtleties of body language can make your dealings with other people easier and more satisfying. In any encounter with someone else, the purpose is communication yet, all too often, the messages we send and receive are unclear at best and contradictory at worst. No matter how well you know someone else, neither of you can really read the other's thoughts, so anything you can do to improve communication is really worthwhile. But before we look at how you can employ your new knowledge in everyday life, think about what you are trying to achieve.

As we've seen, it is possible to use body language to deceive and manipulate other people. There may be occasions when this is what you want to do, but if this is all you do, your skills will be misdirected. The idea isn't to turn yourself into a kind of autocratic stage or film director, controlling the cast of people who are part of your life. Nor is it to turn you into an automaton who uses body language in a calculating way rather than as a spontaneous means of self-expression. Interpreting other people's body language and making sure your own is truly reflecting your intentions and feelings is both fun and genuinely constructive, provided you don't let yourself become too obsessed with it.

ROOM FOR IMPROVEMENT?

Even if you are naturally a good communicator, there are bound to be aspects of your behaviour which could use a little polishing. And for those who have realised that their body language is letting them down, it's worth working out just what's going wrong. Try the quiz below to see where there is room for improvement.

Question

1 At a party do you:
a) spend most of the time with your oldest friend?
b) end up trapped with the biggest bore in the room?
c) get chatted up by everyone except the one you're interested in?

2 At work, do you:
a) get treated like the general dogsbody?
b) find you're the last one to know when your staff make a mistake?
c) have trouble getting your views noticed in meetings?

3 Do your family:
a) take you for granted?
b) treat you like a bit of a joke?
c) take no notice when you're under pressure?

4 Do your friends:
a) rely on you to help them out?
b) fail to give you support when you need it?
c) only see you when it suits them?

5 Is your social circle:
a) all people you've known for years?
b) shrinking?
c) too big for you to have time for everyone?

What your answers reveal

1 a) Why bother going to a party at all? When you're with a good friend, you probably sit or stand quite close together, with your bodies oriented towards one another so no one else feels they can break in even if they want to. Why not try and expand the circle a bit by giving others an opening to join in if they want to? Otherwise you may as well meet your friend somewhere else or simply decide that you're not really a party animal and stay at home.

b) Either you're too soft-hearted for your own good, or you simply don't know how to freeze someone out politely. If you do want to escape, try cutting down the amount of support and prompting you provide as the bore drones on. Should that fail, start looking round the room – anywhere but at your companion – and he or she should get the message.

c) Definitely a signalling failure here. What are you doing to encourage the wrong people – is it your clothes, your manner or your posture? You are somehow giving a misleading impression about the kind of person you are so you need to discover why. Then you can concentrate on attracting the person you are interested in with looks, smiles and a bit of body pointing. It may not work, but it's worth a try!

2 a) Does anyone realise that you're getting all the dumb jobs or that you actually resent it? If you smile and agree meekly they will assume you don't mind. You need to work on looking – and sounding – more assertive. Standing or sitting tall, looking people in the eye and sounding confident are all good for starters. If you don't act submissive, there's much less chance of being treated that way.

b) You need to ask yourself why you are apparently regarded as unapproachable so colleagues let you find things out for yourself instead of coming to tell you. Perhaps your office is particularly forbidding – or perhaps you are. Hiding behind a large desk and/or a closed door, or appearing to be distant or superior, discourages people from telling you what you need to know – especially when it's bad news. Adopting a more open style of behaviour and even just unbending a bit may well improve the situation.

c) Meetings can often be something of a bear pit with everyone fighting to dominate the proceedings so the weakest go to the wall. You need to make an effort to get yourself – and your ideas – noticed without necessarily joining in any pitched battles. As we saw in chapter 2, dressing distinctively helps you to stand out from the crowd, and when you do speak you must say your piece reasonably quickly and without too many qualifications or pauses for interruptions.

3 a) You are only taken for granted when everyone can safely assume that you won't do anything to change the situation. Moderate and routine amounts of moaning are just ignored, so you will need to assert yourself to get everyone to sit up and take notice. Whether you want the kids to tidy their rooms, your partner to appreciate you more or to stop them all treating you as a private, interest-free bank, say so in a way that makes it clear you mean it. Sulks and shouting may have to be accepted calmly and resolutely for a few days, but they'll soon learn that this is a new you and react accordingly.

b) When you're constantly teased or the butt of family jokes, you can get used to it and decide it's not worth making a fuss. Nevertheless, it can become a bit wearing, so if you want them to cut down, make your feelings clear. You've probably developed the habit of laughing at yourself along with everyone else – so try keeping a straight face next time. You may need to go further and leave the room if your expression isn't enough to do the trick, and if you have to actually spell it out, do so firmly without smiling or apology.

c) Perhaps you have become rather too good at hiding your

216

real state of mind. Unless other people can see that you're feeling stressed they won't think to offer help. You can start by trying to offload some of the problems on to other people – just telling them you have too much on and need help may be enough. Remember, though, that most people react negatively to being made to feel guilty, so you'll do better to ask for what you want calmly and positively rather than blaming them for leaving everything to you.

4 a) Helping out is fine provided it doesn't turn into a one-way street. If you've let it go too far, you need to adopt a different manner sometimes when you feel you're being put upon. For example, you can make it clear to a chance caller that you're in the middle of something important or about to go out by limiting the amount of attention you give them instead of responding as though you have all the time in the world. When you're asked to do a favour that's not convenient, say so politely but clearly. Hesitations or excuses just give openings for persuasion and a sweet smile will tempt them to try and get you to give way.

b) You may be one of those who prefer to cope without making a fuss, so your friends don't even know that you have a problem. But if you can unbend enough to let people see that you need help, other people will probably be only too willing to offer it. Instead of minimising any difficulty, don't hide it, and don't be too quick to discourage offers of support or practical help. You've probably learned to control your facial expressions so why not just relax and let your real feelings show?

c) It could be that you've given the impression of being an easy-going person who's quite happy fitting in with their arrangements. If this isn't really the case, it's time you stood up for yourself a bit more. Instead of pleasantly agreeing to whatever is suggested, you can make it clear by your tone of voice and your expression as well as your words when it doesn't suit you.

5 a) You're lucky if you still get on just as well with all of your friends as you did when you first met. Sometimes, though, you stick with people just because you've known them for years, even though you don't really have as much in common as you once did. Ask yourself whether you would like to meet some new people to broaden your social circle and make life more interesting. Taking up new activities and doing things you enjoy with like-minded people can give you the chance to develop other aspects of your personality. It can be a bit daunting getting to know new people when you're out of practice, but if you're open and obviously interested in them, people will mostly respond in kind.

b) You might like to think about why you seem to see fewer people these days. Are you rebuffing them by always seeming to be too busy for them or simply not letting them know that you would like to see them? If you refuse invitations often enough or always seem as if you're anxious to get away, people will assume you're not interested and stop bothering you. You may have to make an effort to focus more of your attention on other people, so that they are in no doubt that you enjoy their company.

c) Most people enjoy feeling that they're popular, but it can get out of hand. Instead of enjoying your relationships, you start to fret that you're neglecting some people, or exhaust yourself in an endless whirl of visits and outings. One way of tackling the problem is to consider which of the people you really want to see. Are there some who have been attracted by your apparent interest in them or your open personality even though you're not actually that bothered about them? You really can't be everybody's friend, so maybe you need to tone down your natural friendliness a little and reserve your warmth for those you really care about.

PRACTICE MAKES PERFECT

As we've said, you don't want to concentrate so hard on body language that your life becomes one long performance. Nevertheless, if you want to hone your skills for specific situations – such as a job interview or to let people see more of the real you – you need to develop some of the same techniques as an actor. The most effective way to do this is to think yourself into the part. As we've seen, some aspects of body language, such as a genuine smile, can't be faked anyway. You can only give off the right signals if they are reflecting how you actually feel. Sometimes, though, this is difficult. For a shy person to smile naturally in a group of strangers may mean they have to produce the emotion from some other source – such as thinking of something pleasant or funny from the past. This is how many actors do it – if possible by relating their character's situation to something they can recognise in their own lives.

You may be feeling that's all very well for Marlon Brando, but not so easy for you. But you can make it easier with a little private rehearsal. Try standing in front of a mirror and smiling in response to a happy memory. Although, as we saw in chapter 3, this kind of smile may not be identical to the one you might produce spontaneously, the difference is subtle. Because it really is a genuine 'enjoyment' smile, you will see that it actually reaches your eyes, and that is the important element as far as other people are concerned.

How much effort you're prepared to put in will depend on how badly you need to get your body language right. For example, if you're facing a crucial job interview, it would be worth actually setting up a role-play situation with a friend as a kind of dry run. You will probably feel a bit silly, but if you take it seriously, you can make sure that you're sitting well, talking in a confident voice and generally coming across positively. Public figures who are trained to look good on TV go through mock-up interviews so they can assess their appearance and body language on the TV screen afterwards. Many are amazed to discover what a difference the way they sit makes or that they have some peculiar mannerisms which look odd on screen.

WATCHPOINTS

When facing an important encounter where you need to come across well, ask a trustworthy friend whether you have any distinctive mannerisms which detract from the impression you want to convey.

Do you:
- Often sit with your head on one side?
- Do a 'Princess Di' and look up at people through your eyelashes?
- Tap with your fingers or feet?
- Slump in a chair rather than sitting straight?
- Fiddle with your watch, ring, or other accessories?
- Constantly touch your face or hair?
- Wave your arms around a lot when you're talking?

None of this is a crime, but it can be distracting for your listener. It probably doesn't matter much most of the time, but it could go against you in a job interview, for example.

This doesn't mean you've got to try and suppress all your spontaneous body language. You would lose a lot of what makes you the person you are, and you couldn't do it if you tried anyway. What is useful is to develop 'body awareness'. There's nothing wrong with using your hands and arms to emphasise or illustrate what you're saying, for instance, and it probably makes you a lively conversationalist. Nevertheless, it's as well to know that you're doing it so that you can tone it down if you feel the occasion requires a less flamboyant approach. A similar principle applies as far as other people are concerned too. While you don't want to focus too hard on details of their body language, you will understand them better if you learn to become aware of it. You'll then be less likely to make mistakes about them. For instance, if your body-language antennae are finely tuned, you'll be able to distinguish between someone who is shy, and someone who simply isn't interested in you and wants to get away. Even more worthwhile perhaps, you'll spot signs of genuine interest even when they are quite subtle.

SEE FOR YOURSELF

If you want to put the theory to the test, try looking out for some of the main signals we've been considering.

- Next time you're having a chat with a close friend, remember to check occasionally on 'mirroring'. Does your posture reflect that of your friend and vice versa? Do you tend to move in unison and copy one another's moves? Don't concentrate too hard on the exercise, just check out your positions now and again when it occurs to you.
- When you're in a room with other people who don't know one another well, take note of how they're sitting or standing in relation to each other. How close are they? What messages can you pick up from the way their bodies are positioned? Look to see whether individual clumps of people are open to outsiders – which way are their feet pointing? You may see signs of people attempting to adjust the distance between them, especially if they don't all come from the same cultural background.

221

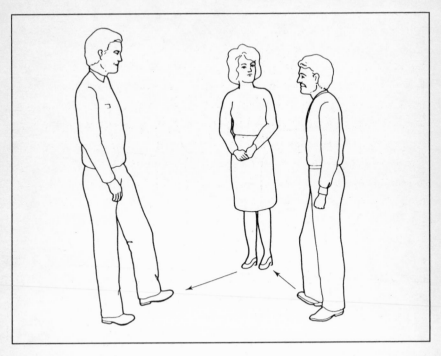

The positioning of feet reveals true desires.

- If ever you're involved in a formal meeting of any kind, look to see how people have arranged themselves in terms of seating. Is there an oblong or oval table with the 'leader' at one end? If so, have the other 'dominant' individuals managed to position themselves close by? Is there anyone who stands out from the rest, because of gender, ethnic origin or dress, and if so, do the others take particular notice of him or her?
- When you're in a pub or restaurant, sneak a look at some of the couples. Have they opted to sit next to one another or on opposite sides of the table? Are they sitting in such a way as to shut out potential intruders? How much smiling and gazing is going on? You need to be a bit discreet about all this observation, but you may be surprised at how much you can deduce.

222

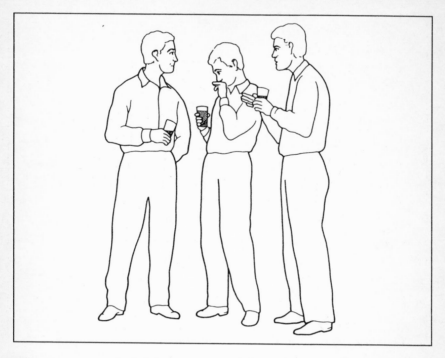

The two men on the left have positioned themselves to exclude the man on the right.

- If you have to persuade a reluctant person to cooperate with you on some task at work or wherever, try sitting alongside them while you explain, and make a point of looking at them and smiling a lot. According to the theory, this is the best way of counteracting hostility or competitiveness, so it's interesting to see whether it works for you.

- After you've spent some time with a person you've never met before, take a moment to consider your impression of them. Did you find them sympathetic, and if so, why? Try and rerun the encounter in your mind's eye, remembering particularly how they looked – especially their posture and facial expressions. Then you can analyse which aspects contributed most to your subsequent feelings about them. For example, you may realise that you felt uncomfortable because the other person stood too close for comfort, or that you instinctively distrusted them because their smiles never reached their eyes.

When you find yourself watching others in this new light, you have begun to develop fluency in a new kind of language – the art of reading, understanding and appreciating non-verbal communication or 'body talk'. People-watching may become an absorbing hobby, a pleasure like listening to music or learning the names of plants and flowers. Not only will this help to pass the time in situations such as station waiting-rooms or lying on the beach, but it will enable you to gain greater rewards in your working and social lives.

Further help

Unfortunately, there is no single or direct route to finding the right kind of help if you feel you might benefit from social skills training. It's more a question of considering the various options which will depend on where you live, whether you can (or choose) to pay for treatment and so on. Before taking up any form of treatment, you should check carefully whether the kind of help on offer will meet your particular needs. Unless you are going through the NHS, ask in advance about costs and how long the course of treatment is likely to last. Some of the avenues you might like to try are listed below.

Psychologists
Clinical psychologists practise in the NHS and privately and those who specialise in cognitive or behavioural therapy may see patients who need help to improve their social skills. Your GP may be able to refer you, or you could contact:

**British Association for Behavioural and
Cognitive Psychotherapies**
Northwick Park Hospital
Watford Road
Harrow HA1 3UJ

Neurolinguistic programming
This sometimes forms part of management training courses and

claims to help you to a clearer understanding of how your behaviour affects other people. Find out more from:

The Association of Neurolinguistic Programming
PO Box No 78
Stourbridge DY8 2YP

Counselling
You will need to check that any counsellor you contact has had the right kind of training and experience as they use a wide variety of approaches, some of which may not be appropriate for you. Your GP may offer counselling in the surgery. If not, or if the service is not suited to your needs, contact:

British Association for Counselling
1 Regent Place
Rugby
Warwickshire CV21 2PJ

Assertiveness training
Courses are quite widely available, often as local authority day or evening classes. Ask at your local library for details.

Recommended Reading

Bodily Communication Michael Argyle, Methuen, 1986 *Psychology for Performing Artists*, Glenn Wilson, Jessica Kingsley, 1994

Body Language: How to Read Others' Thoughts by Their Gestures, Allan Pease, Sheldon Press, 1988

Body Language: Read the Hidden Codes and Maximize Your Potential, Jane Lyle, Hamlyn Publishing Group, 1990

Body Speech, Samy Molcho, Sun Books, 1985

Communicate with Confidence, Dorling Kindersley, 1993

Man Watching: A Field Guide to Human Behaviour, Desmond Morris, Elsevier International Projects Ltd and Jonathan Cape, 1977

Index

229